STEPPING STONES TO THE ARCH DE PLEASURE

Getting Screwed to Your Satisfaction

JAMES POPE

Archway Publishing books may be ordered through booksellers or by contacting:

Archway Publishing
1663 Liberty Drive
Bloomington, IN 47403
www.archwaypublishing.com
844–669–3957

Because of the dynamic nature of the Internet, any web addresses or links contained in this book may have changed since publication and may no longer be valid. The views expressed in this work are solely those of the author and do not necessarily reflect the views of the publisher, and the publisher hereby disclaims any responsibility for them.

ISBN: 978-1-6657-5463-7 (sc)
ISBN: 978-1-6657-5462-0 (e)

Library of Congress Control Number: 2023923885

Print information available on the last page.

Archway Publishing rev. date: 12/15/2023

Readers of the world:

STEPPING STONES to the ARCH De PLEASURE dismisses the fantasy erotic writings such as Fifty Shades and all other imagery erotic written material. Stepping Stones tells the reader realism of day-to-day sexual experiences James Pope has had with women unashamed of their sex needs. The documented sexual situations are with women ages eighteen to seventy-eight. Education ranges from Mensa, PhD, college, and working women. The common thread with all these women is that there desired sexual needs will not go unsatisfied. These women educated me with the fact that there is no such thing as dirty sex. The women's physical actions are very blunt: "If you do not have the ability to satisfy my sexual needs, get out of my bed!"

These are the subjects I will discuss in depth as my life's experiences evolved. Socializing / networking, referral sex, expanding my worldly knowledge, sex with married women, sex and education, car sex I, car sex II, road sex, office sex: hers, office sex: mine, Pope meets Mensa, sex with my mother-in-law, Trifecta - Wednesdays sex, single man in a wife swapping club, three-way-sex, ex-nun-sex, oral sex: giving, oral sex: receiving, real estate sex I, real estate sex II, always be prepared for PERIOD sex, herpes sex, anal sex, international sex I, international sex II, multiple climaxes I, II, and III, piano bar meeting sex I, and piano meeting Sex II.

My standing ovation in the men's room, during intermission of the San Francisco Ballet performance of the Nutcracker!

All week long excitement was building as Gerry and I had opening night, dress circle theatre tickets, for the Nutcracker.

Saturday was here at last! Morning coffee, late champagne brunch.

Afternoon "fun" in our soak N' poke

Lunch on the patio.

Time to dress for the theatre. My tux felt tight, must be gaining weight.

Getting in and setting my 54 Bentley R, my clothes just wasn't comfortable.

During intermission, in the men's room, there were men line at every urinal.

When it was finally my turn, I couldn't find the whole in my underwear..

Men, tired of waiting behind me started jumping to other lines.

Out of desperation I reached in my fly.

To my surprise I had my swim suit on.

I pulled out of line, undressing, all the men were roaring with laughter. There was crowd outside the exit door, everyone laughing, as men told them what happened. Gerry didn't know if she should hide, leave?

**WHO SAID THAT IF SEX IS A PAIN IN THE
ASS, YOU'RE DOING IT WRONG?**

Stepping Stones to the ARCH De PLEASURE
(Getting Screwed to Your satisfaction)

Andy Rooney: Life is like a roll of toilet paper.
The closer you get to the end, the faster it goes.

CONTENTS

WOMEN OF THE WORLD BEWARE!
INTERNATIONAL SEX FIEND ON THE LOOSE

HE'LL RAVAGE EVERY HOLE IN YOUR BODY. HE'LL TICKLE YOUR
CLITORIS TILL IT'S LAUGHING SO LOUD, YOU'LL HAVE TO USE
A PAD TO COVER THE LIPS TO MUFFLE THE SOUND

CAUTION!

INSTRUCTION FOR READING *STEPPING STONES TO THE ARCH De PLEASURE!*

Arch de Pleasure is so hot, asbestos gloves should be worn to protect your fingers from getting burned!

Place an asbestos blanket on your lap when sitting down. If you happen to lay it down without it, the heat may burn through your clothes, setting your pubic hairs on fire. You can purchase insurance from the publisher for coverage.

Reading stands are recommended for hands free gratification.

As I sip my three fingers of 100 proof KNOB CREEK, two cubes, and a splash, I'll began this wondering path looking for sex. There's so much lying around, I just hope I don't step in any. I've heard some of those CENTER CUTS have teeth and bite.

What the hell is this? "Arch de Pleasure" is used to describe the taking away of the RAW edges describing a man giving oral sex. I couldn't come up with unique words to include a soft way to give women credit giving oral sex to be used in the title. I didn't think using "WHEN IT'S MORE THAN A MOUTH FULL or DON'T TALK WHILE YOU'RE EATING ANOTHER CLUB LUNCH really didn't fit what I'm trying say. My normal vocabulary is in colorful terms, such as NAKED LUNCH, CENTER CUT, SNIFF and EAT, PIT STOP. Terms women have used include CLUB, LONG TOM, SUCKED DRY, LICKED THE PLATTER CLEAN, DID THE DISHES, CLEANED THE HOUSE, (don't want any of those tiny ball on the ends of pubic hairs).

At age eighty reflecting on my life, I put together a list of actual sexual situations I have experienced. The core of all situations is TRUE. When writing this revelation (God, sounds like I'm writing a Bible), I used generic locations to protect the women. You'll know when I'm using actual locations.

After reviewing and refining my list, encompassing about more than fifty-five women, I realized I have a fantastic control group. Due to the sexual diversity, this information is too important not to share with the world. I truly do believe this information makes me a sex expert.

True Facts

- Car intercourse with married women: 2-Corvette, 1-Caddy, 1-Lincoln, 1 my office
- Road sex, oral, receiving: 4 different women, guessing 350 miles, trips of 45 miles to across town, several times.
- Car sex, oral giving: 2
- Office sex, hers: 1 woman 3 times
- Office sex, mine: 3 women
- Sex with my mother-in-law: 13 years, too many to count
- Wednesdays Trifecta: guessing 300 times
- Being single in wife swapping club
- Three-way-sex: two women suggested, couldn't find a third
- Ex-Nun sex oral/intercourse: 3 and 3
- Oral sex, giving in bed: too many to count
- Oral sex, receiving in bed: too many to count
- Real estate intercourse: 1 single, 1 married
- PERIODS started while riding in my car: 2 different women
- Herpes safe sex: 1 woman, several times
- Anal sex: 4 women, several times
- International sex: 2 women, several times
- Piano bar meeting ending in intercourse: 3 women

In each situation, I planted plenty of flowers to add fragrance for the bees sniffing for honey. I've had to stop writing several times and find a three hole merchant (woman) as even my fingers would get so hard I could not operate the keyboard. Every time this happened, I found one that could soften the situation that allows me to get back to work. Disability insurance denied.

I caught a segment of Dr. Phil where he arranged a date for a woman who didn't have guts to find help to overcome her shyness so she would be socially confident to ask a man for a date. Let her stay in her world of dildos and self-gratification. Dr. Phil and a dumb so called relationship councilor, arranged a date for a woman to go to an upscale restaurant. Dr. Phil and his incompetent advice guy sat outside in a van, watching her as they give advice on what to say and act - facial expressions, play with hair, let hair down. DUMB! DUMB! DUMB! Date disaster.

Dr. Phil, I wish you, that lady, and I could sit down on your stage and discuss a process with her.

Dr. Phil, I too have a PhD. My PhD is a "Post Hole Digger". I earned it from four women on separate occasions, some three hundred or so miles, blasting down the freeway at 80 mph, middle of the day, receiving oral sex, trucks and pickups buzzing around getting looks, placing my finger to lips, shaking head telling them to keep quiet, making binocular motion with hands in front of my eyes then pointing down, telling them to look but don't disturb. She rises up, mouthing the words to them, "You should be so lucky." I had women liking anal sex better than vaginal sex, motorcycle foreplay, naked pool, and hot tub parties! Three holes, two-hand games and everything sex from A to Z.

Dr. Phil: Those that can, DO! Those that can't, give advice!

Now that you have an idea what I'm about, we'll continue with POLE IN THE HOLE. For those of you that are not ready to leave the world of self-gratification and be vaulted into prime time, we are not talking about your electric company. Continue with your comic books.

I will not use real names as some of these women may still be above ground, fantasizing over their life's sexual path. The names have long escaped me to the ozone. If the names are known and revealed, it may have disastrous effects to their present living arrangements.

I must thank a group of great women in my life as we both taught and learned new ways to achieve greater sexual satisfaction. Men, I'll tell you up front that some things may shock you and some will be left out. I just hope when that happens, those that can embrace it and those that can't, will feel deeply disappointed.

The women's education ranges the full spectrum from Mensa, PhD, college, and working women. The higher the education, the more assertive, demanding and guiding they were. The women range from teens to seventy-eight years old. In bed, the seventy-eight-year-old had all the energy and stamina of a thirty-five-year-old and game for anything.

I'm thankful for the women for taking their time teaching me the finer art of sex and exposing me to the culture. They were all high-energy kick-ass women, comfortable at formal theater openings and bare- ass group swim parties. What wonderful women! What a wonderful life. Unbelievable!

I WILL NOT USE ANY REAL NAMES. I WILL USE THE QUIRKIE NAMES THAT SOME WOMEN GAVE ME!

WHEN I USE THE NAME "PARTNER" or "SHE", IT'S GENERIC FOR THE WOMAN THAT IS WITH ME AT THE TIME

Now that age has rendered the stem end of my bladder useless for sex, it's now nothing more than a flap to keep the flies away from my stinking ass.

Men, if you are not quite ready for prime time, to get the maximum benefit from the *Stepping Stone to the Arch de Pleasure,* read my brochure *Primer for the White Knuckled, Jellied Knee Socializer.* The purpose is to help overcome your social insecurities.

Who could've realized a childhood game we played while I was in the second and third grade would later in life give me the biggest surprise and greatest sexual satisfaction I ever had.

SEX Ed 101 (and I didn't even know what that was).

I lived in a farming area where neighbors helped each other and socialized together. Farm kid's sex education starts at very early age, watching animals breeding and giving birth. So it was normal knowing how you and your brother and sisters came to life and how mom and dad made it happen. To simply put it, we knew what goes where. What I didn't know was that women had holes for solid and liquid waste disposal and a hole for gratification and reproduction.

Evenings when the neighbors would all get together to socialize, all us kids would go off and play. One of the games we played was "lights off, lights on." The boys and girls would pair off. A person would turn the lights off, leave them off for a brief time, and then turn them back on. The object was to try to catch what the couples were doing.

I was in the second grade. There was only one girl my age, so we were always paired off. We didn't know about kissing, so we always tried to get our hands in each other's clothes. She quickly found the stem end of my bladder to play with. I didn't know that a female had more than one hole, so I always stuck my finger in her ass. As I wiggled my finger, she yelled with delight, not objecting. Soon, she and I went off on our own and played our own game of "you play with mine, I play with yours." Surprise! Another hole! We would be uninterrupted and no lights.

Toward the end of my third grade, our family moved to a different town. GAME OVER. Little did I know that years later, fantastic women would revived that game with a little different version. WOW!!!

My booklet: *Primer for the White Knuckled, Jellied Knee Socializer,* tells how my sisters, Bonnie and Frances made sure I knew how to dance so I'd be confident in that aspect of socializing. My dancing ability rapidly dissolved any fear of rejection if refused when asking a girl to dance. When refused, I'd assure her it was my job to make her the best dancing person on the floor.

During high school, I was working on a farm as a hired man, so my socializing was limited to every other Saturday evening. All the towns within thirty-five miles had population of forty-five to fifteen hundred people. The closest city with a swimming pool was forty miles away. I couldn't take the free two-week Red Cross swimming lessons as I had farm work.

I fell in love with one of my classmates, but she didn't like not having me around all the time. She had a different unexplained kind of personality. If you read my novel TRIFECTA, Julia is roughly based on her life.

TRIFECTA WARNING: Three generations of women from the same family had a sexual relationship with the same man!

How does working on a farm as a hired man for four years during high school give you a social advantage? LESSON: Observe! Communicate!

You grow up listening to all the farm sounds. The older you got, the more important the sounds were. Are the sounds the animals make are stressed or content? The milk cows are calling you to milk them. A horse sees you starts neighing, wanting apple or carrot or just wants petting.

OBSERVING: You must be vigilant as to what is going around you. Weeds in the pasture, wind mill blades going around but the pump rod isn't going up and down. A free range chicken is cackling off in the distant tells you she just laid an egg. Better find it before a bull snake does.

When operating machinery, listening and observing demands your strict attention. A strange noise, you see something not working.

No farmer is going to let a sixteen-year-old person with a drug-induced fried brain in ozone land, get on a $350,000 combine.

Communicating with adults: I am injecting relevant information into conversations, offering suggestions and stating concerns.

So, what did I take with me when I left the farm?

The art of listening, observing and communicating, budgeting, and socializing. Also, thanks to my sisters' love for music and dancing. Those were the tools used to enter the adult world of socializing.

FOREPLAY: That's something you did to warm up before the basketball game. Sniffin' mount? Never heard of it? Try it, you'll like it.

Men: In the second paragraph, I said there is something some men would never experience. If you've been circumcised, I don't think you can do this. I'll explain it now and get it out of the way before we blast off down the sexual highway. You'll enjoy the rest of the ride.

In bed with a woman: She had great-shaped breasts and nipples. As foreplay was progressing, I half straddled her. Put the head of my penis against her nipple, pulled the foreskin up over her nipple and massaged her nipple using my foreskin. Her heightened arousal was the reaction as she continued to rub the stem end of my bladder over her breasts. I immediately added this to my foreplay tool box. And what a unique, useful tool it turned out to be.

These are the subjects I will discuss in depth as my life's experiences evolved.

Socializing / Networking

Respect

Dating

Referral sex

Expanding my worldly knowledge

Sex with married women

Sex and education

Car sex I
Car sex II
Road sex
Office sex, hers
Office sex, mine
Pope meets Mensa
Sex with my mother-in-law
Trifecta, Wednesdays sex
Single in wife swapping club
Three-way-sex
Nun-sex
Oral sex, giving
Oral sex, receiving
Real estate sex I
Real estate sex II
Always be prepared PERIOD sex!
Herpes sex
Anal sex
International sex
Multiple climaxes
Piano sex I
Piano sex II

Full of confidence, I hit the road. Itching to see new places, I headed west to the ocean, stopping at Seattle, Portland, Las Vegas, Santa Barbara, Los Angeles, and San Diego and interesting places along the way. Observing my surroundings, it became obvious I needed to change my image. I was certain my old Chevy was holding me back. I paid cash for a new Corvette. I was always drawn to places of music and dance. A gal I met at a dance told me I needed to update my wardrobe, my Iowa farm clothes didn't fit in. She took me under her wing and helped me buy the kind of clothes I needed. A three-piece suit, casual wear, and John Deere tractor just didn't go together. No attraction for either of us. Keep looking.

I soon found out I only graduated with "Intelligence come Lott a."

What is sex? Sex is nothing more than a body function fulfillment. There is no such thing as dirty sex. You must always be thinking outside the "box." Her body responses to your probing and audible utterances will be our guide. She may do the guiding.

Referral Sex: Only satisfying performance needed.

I learned how important it is to be positive, outgoing and respectful. Wonderful things can happen if you are a decent person.

Before I knew I didn't know anything about mature sex, my first adult sexual experience was handed to me. A coworker asked me to come by his house after work for a drink. I had attended their wedding. His wife was a lot of fun joining in the conversation. Visiting, drinking, a knock on the door, and a nice looking woman walked in. She was a neighbor. I was introduced to her. She saw my Corvette and wanted to know who owned it. She stayed to visit and have a drink. I walked her outside for her to get a closer look at the Vette and sit behind the steering wheel.

The next day, my friend explained that the woman's husband just got a big promotion and now thinks his wife wouldn't fit the image he needed.

A couple of days later, my friend tells me, "For lunch, go to my house, the neighbor gal would like to see you." At his house, the neighbor woman was there. His wife says, "Lunch is in the fridge, I've got some errands to run, be back in a couple of hours."

My first adult sex, a naked lunch with a married woman all in one day! The four of us went out one evening and upon returning home she wanted to go for a night ride. We found a secluded place and had sex in that Corvette. The only thing I did was undress her and perform. She could tell I was very inexperienced and guided my hands. I HAVE ARRIVED!!

I have a Corvette now. Every time I go into the garage and gaze at the Vette, I remember everything about having sex with that woman. Her smell, her touch, her laugh. What do you suppose she thinks every time she sees a Corvette? Sex in a Vette. Not much room for foreplay. Foreplay wasn't needed.

Our relationship was short lived. The company her husband worked for transferred him to the East Coast. I never heard from her again. My friend, his wife, and I were lifelong friends. I attended their wedding and both of their funerals.

Now, I'm tooling around in the Vette ready to make things happen. There are three kinds of people: those that make it happen, those that let it happen, and those stumbling around saying "What the fuck's happening man?"

I was in social setting, milling around on the fringe of a group of college kids. I heard one of them say a funny name followed by the word screw. Screw! That got my attention. I want to know as much as I can about screwing. I waited until I could talk to the guy alone. I asked him what kind of position that funny screwing was. He laughed telling me, "It's not sex, it's an Archimedes Screw. It's a device invented in Roman time, used to lift water from one level up to the next level." Is this a case of not believing everything you hear?

SOCIALIZING

The only thing I was truly confident with was dancing and music. So I always sought out places with live music. As I observed the dance floor, they were doing something other than waltzes and polkas. My dancing ability wasn't going to help. I went to a dance studio and signed up for every type of dances they taught. Soon enough, I was proficiently dancing to any music the band played. I had no problem approaching women to ask for a dance. If there were women sitting together at a table, I'd ask each of them for a dance. If a woman refused, I'd assure her it was my job to make her the best dancer on the floor. It didn't take long, and I was talking to very interesting women telling me all their interests, everything from culture events to shooting pool and drinking beer.

The first woman who took me to bed and after what I thought was great sex, was very frank with me. She said something like, "You have to slow down. I got no enjoyment and you're finished. Sex is for both of us." I was a failure. After I got dressed and was leaving she said, "I enjoyed your company. Come back tomorrow after work. You can take me out for a nice dinner and afterwards, I'll show you what pleases me." I said, "You make the reservations and don't worry about the cost."

We had a very nice white-table cloth dinner, great slow dance music, and late evening drive in the Vette. At her house, a short drink, setting close, gently touching, and softly kissing. She got up, not saying a word, took my hand and led the way to the bedroom. "Last night, I undressed myself, tonight you undress me, and I undress you. If you see anything you'd like to touch, I'd like that." In bed, she said, "Talk very softly and slowly." Guiding my hands over her body touching her sensitive spots, "Tell me what you're thinking."

As I caressed her body I gently fingered her anus. She didn't object. She guided my head to her breasts. She moved me into position, cleared the hair from the opening and helped guide me into her. Her jerking body, verbalizing shouts, and exhausted lifeless body was a testament of success.

We laid down side by side, holding, caressing, speaking softly. After a trip to the bathroom, I said, "I don't want to forget what you taught me so we'd better do it again." It does take a while to reload so there was ample time to talk, hold, caress. After another trip to the bathroom, I got dressed. She put on her robe, handed me a note, and walked to the door. A kiss goodnight and the door closed behind me. Sitting in the Vette before I started the engine, I read the note. "I love being with you. Please call soon."

Dancing and music was always my ticket to meeting women. After showing sincere interest on their other areas of entertainment, I never hesitated to ask them to expose me to those areas. Man! My social world exploded. I pay you, guide the way. Being sincere, interested, and financially able, these women took me on the most fantastic educational entertaining ride.

POPE MEETS MENSA

Remember, I'm the guy who graduated high school with "Intelligence come Lott a."

I'm at a country western bar, enjoying live shit kick n' music, asking women to dance and having a ball when a nice-looking, nice-build woman, approached me, "I've been watching you and I won't leave here before I get to dance with you". I lead the way to the dance floor. We did a "jitter bug" that was just fantastic. Couples walked off the floor and stood on the side to watch us. When the dance was over, the place exploded with applause. After acknowledging their applause, I said to her, "Let me buy you a drink, and we need to talk." After she spoke the first few sentences, I was blown away. Her conversation was so intelligent and so far above me I just sat in amazement. I told myself, "Shit! I'm dead, nothing here for me." During our conversation, she told she was divorced, had children, and was back attending college. I asked who takes care of the children while she goes out.

"A friend. We swap kid duties so each could have a free night."

FREE NIGHT! Now that got my attention. "Breakfast?"

"Sure, I'm free until morning."

Over breakfast, the conversation was exciting and stimulating. She brushed her hand and a long narrow scar on the side of her cheek could be seen. She then said, "A gift from my ex-husband." I could tell her self-esteem was suffering.

"We've got a lot more things to talk about. You've got a free night. Let's go to my apartment".

"Should I follow you?"

"Is your car parked in a safe place?"

"Yes". It's street parking for my guests. Ride with me, I'll bring you back later."

At my place, she didn't resist my hands on her body and encouraged long kisses.

She stood up, "I need to go to the bathroom. You get the bed ready!"

In bed, I was working my way through the foreplay tool box. When I got to the "lights on, lights off tool" and gently fingered her anus, she hollered, screaming, "Yes! Yes! Put it in!"

I pushed my finger deeper, she was screaming with delight. I withdrew my finger and inserted the stem end of my bladder. She went wild, tarring up the bed, and violently jerking. Exhausted, her body went limp. Recovering, she grabbed me, hugging, and kissing.

"God that was great. Did it bother you?"

I answered, "What pleases you, pleases me." My mind was in shock, reeling!

She asked, "Do you think anal sex is dirty?"

My response was, "No. In fact the tightness gave me heightened pleasure. Before I leave, we'll do it your way."

"NO. Your way works for me."

Who said, "If sex is a pain in the ass, you're doing it wrong?" My answer, "Try it, you'll like it."

Coming out of the bathroom wearing an open bathrobe gave me full frontal view of that gorgeous body. Her voice low and soft, "Jim, when I saw you naked, I was amazed how big you were, then you got an erection. I didn't know if I should be shocked or thrilled. I've never experienced anything that big".

Hmm. A new tool for, I can't call foreplay, an afterplay tool box.

I was telling her how I admired her intelligence and asking if she knew just how intelligent she was. Her college was about forty miles away. She was nearing the end of her second year. She called me, asking if I'm free time tomorrow.

"Yes, I can get away."

"I've only one class tomorrow morning. How about going with me?"

Me go to college? "Yes, sounds interesting," was my response.

The class was about management. The professor asked the class their views about management. The class had a lot of low-paying-part-time-job students. All were giving negative examples of helicopter, abusive, and authoritarian.

The professor pointed to me and said, "We'll ask our guest his views."

I stood up and answered, "The only work that gets done is what is inspected to get done. Not expected to get done. A manager is responsible for providing proper training. Assign work, observe and help the employee in ensuring they can do the work correctly, offering positive feedback. Once trained of assign work, instruct the employee to report when the job is finished. The manager inspects the work. If it's done correctly, he gives the employee positive feedback. If it's not correct, more training. The manager should create a brag folder for the employee. The manager documents all good and bad things about the employee. The employee also puts things in his brag folder, what he/she does outside of work that will aid in his annual evaluation. This makes it very easy for a manager when writing evaluations and promotion consideration.

Two things I want you to write down, memorize it, and brand in your brain. It will serve you well. THERE IS NO SUCH THING AS A PROBLEM. A PROBLEM IS NOTHING MORE THAN A QUESTION THAT NEEDS TO BE ANSWERED!

An employee comes rushing to you, "Boss I got a problem, it won't work." You say, "Wait, take a deep breath and calm down. What's happening?"

"The gizzy which is the wrong type and won't go into the flapper dunk!"

Manager, "Let me make sure I understand what's happening. It's a gizzy which to flapper dunk connecting, is that the question?"

"Yes"

"Well let's find the answer to the question."

A PROBLEM CAUSES HYSTERIA. A QUESTION INVOKES THOUGHT, PROBLEM SOLVING.

A person cannot grow without criticism! You must welcome, embrace differing points of view. Learn from it. If you're a right fighter, you're a looser".

I sat down, the room was silent. The professor said, "It takes me four months to teach what you covered in a few sentences. Do you have a management degree?"

"Yes, I have a PhD. My PhD is *post hole digger*. I earned it during my four years of high school, working on a farm as a hired man. The room bursts out in laughter.

The professor said, "Next time, come back as a guest speaker."

At the end of the class the students wanted to talk and shake my hand.

DEAR MOM,
I TAUGHT A PROFESSOR SOMETHING TODAY!

Heading to her home forty miles away, we stopped to grab a bite and hit the freeway.

"You keep telling me how intelligent I am but you amaze me."

I said, "You're not interested in knowing how intelligent you are?"

"I've been thinking about it." Her hand was resting on my leg, softly rubbing it, unzipping my pants and started playing with the stem end of my bladder. Of course, it got hard! She raised up the seat arms, laid her head in my lap, pulled out the stem end and started the mouth works.

WOW! Middle of the day, at seventy miles an hour, I was experiencing oral sex. All I could do was gently brush her hair and neck. A REALLY, REALLY, BIG, FEEL-GOOD experience. Trucks and pickups would pull up beside us. When someone looked down into my car, I'd put my finger to my lips indicating to look but be quite. Some vehicles would slow down, drop back, and come up on the other side so the other person could see. The changing of engine sound made her turn her head sideways asking what's happening.

I replied, "The other person is getting a look."

"I won't have time when I get home, so this will satisfy both of us."

The oral sex continued until we reached her exit. As she was putting the stem end back in my pants, she kissed it saying, "There all squeaky clean."

We made arrangement to attend opening theatre night. Formally dressed, we looked great.

She then said, "I've got exciting news! I'm MENSA qualified. The college made the arrangements for the test."

I was elated, "What can I do special for you?"

"Let me sleep on it, I'll think about it. Of course, I think better with you in my bed."

After the performance, we went to a small, intimate café for drinks and some toad in the hole.

Midnight, on the freeway heading to her place, she suddenly screamed, "PULL OVER! STOP! My period is starting!"

"I don't have any protection. Do you have a towel?"

My mind was racing, "No, only a shine rag in the trunk."

"GET IT!"

Back in the car, I handed her the rag. "Help me, I can't get my dress and slip up past my knees." Successful in getting the rag inside her pantyhose and in place, the rest of the drive was rather quite.

Boy, the jobs a person gets tasked with! At her house, walking her to the door, she said, "All I want to do is get cleaned up and go to bed. I'll make it up to you."

Little did I know that wouldn't be the last time I'd be the COVER PERSON. And that's the end of that.

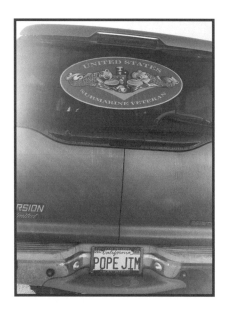

MENSA CONNECTION: I was in a relationship with MENSA 1979. The photo above is the back of my 2000 Ford Excursion. MENSA gave me that license plate as birthday gift. At the time I put it on my Ford station wagon, than a Lincoln Town car, Mercides 450SL, Chevy Sunburn, now no my 2000 Ford excursion.

MENSA GONE, but not forgotten! 44 YEARS!

PERIOD

Work sent me to a very large city. It was evening in my hotel room, I was reading the newspaper, and saw in the entertainment section something that look interesting but had no idea what it was. My immediate thought was to call MENSA.

"MENSA, help. There's a theatre group from England, the Oily Cart Players, ever heard of them?"

"Spell it."

"It's D Oily Cart Players?"

"They're doing a bunch of Gilbert and Sullivan stuff."

"Oh my God! They're the gold standard performers of G&S Operettas. You have to see them. Don't leave until you do."

"If I fly you in will you see it with me?"

"Yes, yes."

I am now hooked on Gilbert & Sullivan.

After some great screaming, tearing-up the bed sheets sex, lying, catching our breaths after arousing round of hole poking, I said, "I've got the answer for the next time we're together when the sex urge hits us and you're having your period. It's called two hands, three holes."

She asked, "What's that?"

"You have two hands and three holes, cover the two you don't want used!"

She slapped me! Laughing, she said, "I can see that happening."

MENSA and I had the greatest of times. Circumstances dictated I must move on and relocate.

Sitting, thinking, and bunch of junk going through my mind, the Boy Scout motto "Be Prepared" came to the surface through all the stuff. Thinking about it, I went out and purchased a few tampons and pads placing them in paper sack in the trunk of my car. Thank God, I did. They came in very handy. I called them "MAN HOLE COVERS."

While we're on the subject of anal sex, I'll go ahead and cover the other three situations.

POPE, MEETS WILD ONE

I became very good friends with a couple. I treated the three of us to many nights socializing. The husband was a woman chaser. He had a part-time job at a gas station. He would have women come to the gas station. He'd put the car on the hoist, they would get in the car, then the other attendant would hoist the car up high and they would have sex.

His company sent him overseas to one of their jobs. His wife had a feeling he was cheating, so I didn't have a problem asking her out. She was part Cherokee Indian, drop-dead gorgeous, she'd make Cher look like a poster child for ugly. She welcomed me, taking her and her three children out and paying the babysitter so we could go out.

I took her to a hypnotist show. We were sitting close to the back. As the hypnotist was going through his routine with the people on stage, Indian started feeling the effects and going under the spell. She recovered and didn't remember anything. On the way home, we stopped to grab something to eat. Stopping in her driveway, I started getting out of the car. She grabbed my arm.

"Sit and hold me." Full-on foreplay. "I'll send the sitter home, the kids are in bed. We'll finish this in the house."

We were in bed like a flash. Even Santa Clause would be pleased with our speed. I'm zipping through my tool box full of foreplay secrets. Then, I stopped to smell and sniff the arch of pleasure. Her body fragrance was so alluring it pulled me in. I pulled up a seat at the arch and ate my fill. Moving on to the next foreplay tool, my magic finger, I gently fingered her anus.

"Yes!" she screamed, pulling a pillow over her head to muffle her wanting cry. Boy, did I know this drill. I inserted and held on as her violent jerking did the work.

Our next outing was a pub crawl. She was dressed in skin-tight jeans and form-fitting blouse. When the music stopped for intermission, off we went to the next bar, having a different kind of music. We'd make four stops a night. We ended up several miles from her house. Late night, on the freeway, 75 mph in the fast lane, she let out a scram, "GET OFF THE ROAD! STOP THE CAR!"

"What's the matter?"

"I'm starting my period! I've got nothing with me!"

"I got it covered, I have a magic sack in the trunk."

Back in the car, I handed her the sack.

"I can't get my jeans down to get my legs far enough apart."

Being a good Boy Scout, I helped get her jeans and panties down below keens. She got a tampon inserted and while she was pulling up her panties I said, "Here, slap this *MANHOLE COVER* on for added protection."

That broke the tension. We both broke out laughing. To hell with getting the panties and jeans pulled up. I knew when she has her periods they were gushers. Almost to the point of having manhole covers delivered by FEDEX. When we got home, she said, "The two-three game?"

And that's the way that night went. Just another PERIOD of time!

The husband came home flat broke. He confided in her that he spent all the money on sex and booze, blaming her for him being lonely and forced him to cheat. I knew that was bull shit! The wife had to get a job to support the family. He became very depressed.

On a Saturday, I went to their house. She was at work. Husband and I sat, hashing over old times. He got up and said, "I'm going to soak in the tub."

I sat at the kitchen table and wrote some letters. After an hour and a half, I knocked on the bathroom door, "Are you OK?"

"Yes, I'm just relaxing" he answered.

A half hour or so later, the wife came in from work. "Where's my husband?"

"He's in the bathroom, relaxing in the tub. He's been in there for about three hours."

She knocked on the bathroom door, "You OK?"

A low gruff voice answered, "Get the kids out of the house!" She tried the door but it was locked. I rounded up their three sons and took them next door to the neighbors. When I got back, she was still trying to get the door open. I kicked it in, blood everywhere. He was sitting in a tub of bloody water, arms resting on each side of the tub. Both wrists had large cuts and when the veins collapsed, he dug at the gashes trying to open them. She was in shock but functioned fairly well.

I called 911. First responders took him out of the house. She left with the EMTs. The neighbor woman came in, seeing the bathroom said, "I'll be right back."

She came back carrying a fifth of HILL & HILL.

"Jim, it's up to you and me to clean this up." We gathered up cleaning gear and entered the bathroom, wedging the door shut. She opened H&H took a sip, handed it to me. I took a sip and sat it on the sink. We scrubbed and sipped. Two hours later, the bathroom was clean and the H&H was gone. She waited while I went over to her house and got the boys. We explained to them their dad was very sick. They inspected the bathroom, finding a speck of blood. I told them their dad was throwing up blood, falling flinging his arms around trying to grab something, falling into the tub. No more questions about it from them.

That night, I sat on a straight back beside her bed, holding her hand all night.

He recovered. Lost his security clearance and placed in a non-classified job. They divorced. He never did fully recover. I remained friends with him till his death. I attended his funeral.

I asked her how she discovered liking anal sex? "My neighbor taught me!"

Hmm, how do you teach a woman to like anal sex better then vaginal sex?

I happened to talk to one of the sons years later. He wanted to know what the bell was for that ran between the two houses. I didn't tell him it was a signal for the neighbor man to come over and poke his mom in her ass. I don't if her husband was screwing the neighbor man's wife. I asked her son where his mom was now.

He said, "She's a drunken slut living in Northern California."

I was with two other women with differing views about anal sex. One woman told me if it helps her get married, she would have vaginal sex during her period, anal sex, and give oral sex. I'll pass on the period center cut entrée. I ran as fast as I could!

The other woman said, a man could anything with her body as long as it pleased him. One-way sex is no fun. I'm outta here.

There was only two other women, other than the four mentioned above that fingered my ass during foreplay. I did not like it but it excited them.

You asked, did I like oral sex? The answer is a **BOLD YES**. But the center cut must pass the smell test and there cannot be any tiny ball clinging to the ends of her pubic hair. In that situation, move to nipples!

Thinking about recent experiences, I stopped by the auto parts store and bought a bundle of shop rags. The next time I'll be stuffing a rag in a THONG.

INTERNATIONAL SEX I

I was transferred to Hawaii. The company shipped my Corvette. My job required travel out of the country. On one of my trips, I met a nice-looking office administrator. We became close, very fast. Telling her about Hawaii and showing her pictures, she saw a picture of my Corvette by a sunny beach. She gushed, "Oh, I'd love to go there someday."

We socialized together and bounced back and forth between her apartment and my hotel room. She was refreshing and exciting.

In my novel **Trifecta,** on page 30, you'll read where I'm in a night club with her and called a serviette a napkin causing the table to explode in laughter and stifled embarrassment.

It was all too soon to have to leave. Saying goodbyes to "My hours in Hawaii are very flexible. If you ever get a chance, please come to Hawaii."

A letter arrived and viewing the post mark my heart started pounding.

"Is the invitation still open? I'm taking a job in London and can spend a month with you on my way."

She loved riding around in the Vette with the top off. She wore sundresses with full skirts. She had long legs and every time she stepped out of the Vette, she put one leg out purposely letting her legs spread wide apart and making sure her skirt pushes high up on her thigh and she would give me a naughty laugh saying, "Leg show."

I'd reply, "Arch De Pleasure."

I took her to my favorite afternoon watering hole, Davy Joes Locker. It was in the center of the underground parking structure at the REEF HOTEL. The hotel sat right on the beach. When the swimmers got out of the ocean, they would do a quick fresh water shower and jump in the swimming pool. Behind the bar was a massive plate glass window that looked out into the deep end of the swimming pool. On the pool side was a ledge at the bottom of the window where swimmers, when getting out of the water, would stand on the ledge and "adjust" themselves. It was always a great show watching what swimmers did adjusting themselves.

My partner was blushing and giggling, "My friends will never believe this."

I said, "Pictures don't lie, take plenty."

A waitress took a stack of business-sized cards and exited the bar. I went to the bar, picked up one of the cards, and handed it to my partner. As she read, she was trying to stifle her laughter. The card reads:

Anyone that takes off their bathing suit bottom and waves it above their head gets a free drink at Davy Jones Locker!

Watching all those guys and gals getting out of their suit bottoms and standing in front of the window naked then getting back into their suit was almost too much for my partner.

"Getting enough pictures?"

Handing me the camera she blasted off the restroom.

Soon people with cards in their hands entered. When they saw the window, they turn around and run out. My partner leaned close to my ear. "I think we should go to your apartment. I don't have a bathing on suit but I do have panties. If you'll help, I'll buy a drink."

"I'll have a double shot of **Panty Remover.** I'll give you a demonstration of my no hands trick."

She said, "I'm trying to get you in bed and you're not using hands?"

"I remove panties with my teeth. Might pull a few hairs but you got plenty."

"Is it OK if I'm laughing while getting screwed?"

"Don't worry. I've got just the thing to keep your mouth busy!"

By now we're laughing uncontrollably. Back at the apartment, sitting side by side, laughing and joking about the day's events.

"Did you get a picture of that man with the stubby dick?"

"I must have. I took a lot of pictures. I know I got one of the gal with the tampon string."

Laughing, she got up heading to the bathroom, "I don't know how much more of this I can take."

When she came out of the bathroom, all she had on was her panties. She was carrying her clothes and dumping them on a chair. She took a stern stance in front me.

"The house is clean. The meal I prepared has the aroma of freshly baked cini buns. Dinner is served at the Arch De Pleasure. Now, set the table with no hands!"

I just sat, gazing at her body, "Get off your ass. Dinner's getting cold. You don't want warm ups, do you?"

I got up, walked around behind her, knelling, I put my mouth on the middle of her back, kissing as I went down. Getting the band of her panties with my teeth, I gently pulled them down part way. I playfully bit her buttocks. I moved around in front of her. Getting the panties in my teeth I pulled them down to her center cut, pausing, "What's the hold up? If you wait any longer, I'll go in the bathroom and masturbate."

"I stopped to smell the ah, ah, roses. You passed the smell test."

Panties off, we moved to the horizontal table. *LET THE FEAST BEGIN.* To prevent conversation while eating I kept her mouth busy. For desert, we did the conventional stuff.

My Vette was a hard top, which was easily removed. When driving around, you had to watch out for sudden brief showers and know where you could quickly get undercover. Davy Jones Locker has saved me many times.

We did all the major islands taking in all what Hawaii has to offer.

All too soon, it was time to say goodbye. Packing to leave, I ask her, "Will we ever be together again?"

She became stone cold somber. She took my hand, pulling to sit beside her on the bed.

"No. I'm engaged to an officer on a cruise ship. We'll be married when I get to London. We'll live on the ship. If I knew you and I would soon be man and wife, I'd call off the engagement. Knowing that will never happen, I must go. If there was even a chance I could live here with you until I could get establish I'd give it a shot. I'm really second guessing my marriage decision." Taking her hands in mine, I said, "My life is always in a state of flux, the company moves me to wherever there's a hole that has to be plugged."

She said, "Well, this is goodbye. This will be the saddest night of my life. Hold me tight while I cry."

I dropped her off at the cruise ship terminal. Sad kisses. Her last words, "I'll be thinking about you and Davy Jones Locker and my great Hawaii memories."

I watched her as she walked up the gangway. On board she turned, and mouthed the words, "I love you," blew me a kiss, waved, turned and was out of sight.

I did get one letter telling me I will always be with her in memory and a "Please don't contact me" note on it.

Same heritage as the one above, but from a different country.

INTERNATIONAL SEX II

I walked out of the International Market Place. When I got to my Vette, there was a gal, late 20s early 30s, standing by it.

"I love your car," she said.

"You live in the islands?"

"I'm here from Texas enjoying Hawaii."

Then I asked the gal, "How long are you here for?"

"I'll be here for another week. Do you know of a good place to have a drink in the afternoon?" My reply was, "I think I know a place you'd enjoy. Hop in. It's just a few blocks away."

I pulled into the underground parking lot at the Reef hotel.

"Oh no, I've had enough of hotel bars," she gasped.

I told her, "Trust me. You'll like this one."

Entering Davy Jones Locker, my gal friend saw the window behind the bar and froze, half hiding her head but peeking.

So I asked her, "You see some exciting things as guys and gals "adjust" themselves?"

She just stood there, hand over her mouth, speechless.

"This is nothing," I continued. "Wait until the show starts."

When the waitress left with the cards, I retrieved one from the bar and gave to the gal I was with.

Reading it, she let out a gasp, "Is this for real?"

My only response was, "Get your camera ready."

She didn't know whether to hide her face, turn her back, or pee her pants. After the show was over, she just sat, motionless.

"I don't think I'll ever recover. Can we take a drive in your Corvette?"

"Yes. I know a place. It's a little far out."

"What's the name?" she asked.

"The place is Pearl City. They have a bar, Pearl City Tavern, that's a good place to just sit and observe. I'll forewarn you, they have some guys and girls that fight like animals. They won't bother you as long as you're with someone. They do a lot of fighting among themselves."

So we walked in at Pearl City Tavern and my friend stopped and started laughing. Running the full length behind the bar was a cage with monkeys. You can't help laughing, watching them. My gal friend just sat shaking her head.

In the car heading back to Honolulu, she asked, "Where do you live? Before I give you your tour guide fee, I like to see how a person lives that can afford a car like this".

Entering my condo she said, "I need to use the bathroom." So I pointed the way and went to the bar and waited for her to come out before I poured us a drink.

I heard the bathroom door, looked around and my eyes fell when I saw that gorgeous tanned figure, wearing only an aqua thong. She then said, "I'm ready to pay my debt in full."

A mental picture flashed through my mind of my shop rag roll lengthwise, stuck through the thong, just above the pleasure pit, like a MUSTACHE.

I took her to Luau show for dinner. She spent the night with me and two more nights before she had to leave.

I sit here with my typewriter, I search the keyboard for the words to express my humble gratitude to all the truly amazing, intelligent women, who allowed me into their lives. With their strength and guidance, we shared the highest of pleasures to the raw exposure of life's necessities. To every one of them, everything is normal and we were able to laugh together at the highs and lows.

I've had two country Western Bands. Country music songs are filled with love and sorrow. When I hear them, a flood of mixed emotions consumes me as I relate.

Does this sound like the end of the story? Not even close. There's still a lot of F-CK-NG (want to buy a vowel), to be done. Read on.

TRAVEL LOG

(A Break from Sex)

It was in the middle of summer. Where my partner and I lived, the temperature was 105. My partner said she'd like us to go somewhere it's a little cooler for a short stay. I made arrangements for an eight-day trip to Russia in January. For the trip, I took 6 dozen ounce bottles of Jack Daniels, 250 one dollar bills, and a gross of Paper Mate pens.

Getting off the plane in St. Petersburg, it was freezing cold, snow axle deep to a Ferris wheel. I went to the men's room. The toilet seat was broken, leaning up against the wall. Welcome to modern Russia.

I told my interpreter Suzanna Bagdasariayan, I wanted to go where the locals go conducting their daily business to observe. We entered a grocery store. The store was packed with shoppers. The checkout clerks were in a raised platform in the middle of the room. Suzanna picked up a one-pound jar of coffee from the shelf.

"Jim, this one-pound jar cost $3.50, a Russian's monthly sociality security is $5.50. We drink small amounts from small cups."

I said," Yep," And everyone around me burst out in laughter.

Walking down the street, there were a lot of people queued up, waiting for the store to open.

"Jim, today, this store advertised chickens. There will be very few chickens and it will be an all-out fight trying to get one."

I said, "Yep!" All the people burst out with laughter.

At the Moscow Hotel, there are security guards at the entrance.

"Jim, the cocktail lounge is in on the second floor. If you go there, be very careful. It's full of women pickpockets and prostitutes. They pay the guards to let them in. They only go as far as the lounge area."

Of course, my partner and I had to go there. The lounge was two rooms. One room had chairs and love seats occupied by several women. In the cocktail lounge, we were dancing. I said to my partner,

"When were you ever on a dance floor and you were the only one that's not a prostitute?"

Laughing she said, "You're paying for everything. Does that make me a whore?"

In the cocktail lounge, there were tables of locals drinking vodka. In the middle of the table sits a big jug of Pepsi they were suing to chase the vodka. I ordered a shot of vodka to see what it tastes like. It was horrible.

Coming out of the hotel's convenience store, walking to the elevators, a drop-dead gorgeous woman fell in step with me. At the elevators, she asked, "Going up?"

I said, "Yep."

She said, "Aren't you going to the lounge?"

"No, I'm going up to my room".

She punched out and left.

I told Suzanna about what happened. "When the woman asked if I was going up, I said 'yep.' We got on and she asked if I was going to the lounge. When I said no, she punched out and left. As I was relaying the story, Suzanna started smiling.

"Jim, when you answered *yep* you told her you wanted to have sex."

"Sex?" I questioned.

Suzanna explained further, "In Russian, *YEP* is slang for wanting to have sex. Remember in the grocery, in front of the department store?"

"You mean, I'm going all over Russia asking everyone if they want to fuck, you want to fuck?"

"That's right," she said.

"Why didn't you correct me?"

Suzanna replied, "You mentioned as we walked the streets how the people walked stooped shoulder, heads down, no hope in their faces? If I could give them a good laugh that might help their spirits, so be it."

I smiled, nodding my head and said, "Anything to help further US-Russia relations."

I overheard people saying they were going to see where the movie *Gorky Park* was filmed.

I said, "Get a ticket to Helsinki, that's where it was filmed. Russia wouldn't give permission for the filming." Talk about astonished people.

I used the booze, money and pens to hand out tips to deserving people. One day, as we were preparing to go out and walk about, my partner asks me to carry her fanny pack as it was so bulky under her heavy coat. On a street corner, there was a large, portly police officer. My partner asked if she could have a picture with him. I took the picture and was digging in her fanny pack for something to give him when my partner yelled, "Jim, watch what you're doing!" Stunned, looking around, she yelled again, "Your hands, your hands!" I had sanitary pads in both hands.

SUNDAY! CHURCH DAY! At the hotel tourist desk, I signed us up for the Sunday morning tour of the Red Square and inside the Kremlin walls. We visited the big GUM department store. Touring inside the Kremlin walls across this wide expanse (which we were not allowed to get closer to), I saw what I thought I was looking at the ends of ricks of PVC.

Pointing I asked, "Suzanna, are they remodeling that building?"

"No, those are cannon barrels captured from Napoleon." No history there.

We entered the Cathedral of the Assumption. This is the Cathedral where Ivan the Terrible was exiled from the church after he sent his fourth wife to a convent. Because he was the head of the country, he could not be kept out of the building. The church built a wooden corral for him. Ivan was allowed to enter through a side door and enter his corral.

We all stood in amazement at the beauty. Brilliant icons covered the walls. Standing, savoring the surroundings, I approached a retired minister in our group.

"This is a once in a life time event. It's Sunday, why don't you quietly ask the tour members if they would like to go over in a corner and in their own way, pause and silently reflect on things you are thankful for."

He stepped away a few feet. Soon he returned.

"No, I don't feel comfortable doing that."

I said, "Hell my name is POPE! I'm qualified to hold communion on airplanes with a jug of Ripple and a bag of croutons. I'll hold church service." I went through our group, inviting them to the corner of the cathedral. Everyone, plus a few extra, including the minister followed me. I received many, many thanks for having the foresight to do it.

There were three older women staying together in a room. They knew the room was bugged. They tore the room apart looking for it. They pulled the rug back and saw a box with wires. They knew they'd found the bug. They worked and worked to get a nut unscrewed. When they did, their bug disappeared through the floor. Bewildered, they lost their bug.

They answered a loud banging on the door. Opening it, the hotel security and police burst in. The women had unbolted the chandelier, and it crashed on the floor in the ballroom down below.

While shopping, I purchased an envelope of souvenirs out-of-circulation postage stamps. I had a stack of post cards to be mailed. The post office in the hotel told me it would cost $2.50 for each post card. I figured it would cost me over sixty dollars. I took my package of stamps I'd purchased, stuck a stamp on each post card and dropped them in the outgoing box. Every post card arrived. I figured it costed me one-sixteenth of a cent per post card.

Added note: A Big Mac at Moscow's McDonalds was 70 US cents.

All must come to an end. At the airport, flight departures are not rigid. We boarded our Helsinki flight as soon as we arrived. We waited a long time for arriving flights connecting passengers.

We had three days before the flight home, to tour. Yes, we saw where *Gorky Park* was filmed, The Copper Church, and as much as we could cram in. A Big Mac costed $8.00 and a Filet-o-Fish, $7.00.

I asked our tour guide, "We heard so much about your educational system in the US. What about it that makes it great?"

The response that I got was, "A child in the first-grade studies our native language. In the second grade, they study a second language and our native language. In the third grade, they study a third language. For the next nine years, they study all three languages. To graduate from high school, a student must be proficient in all three language aspects: speaking, reading, and spelling."

I was in the hotel's convenience store and was approached by a very attractive woman.

"Would you like some company?"

I was not interested as I brought my own with me. "How much?" I asked.

She answered, "Three hundred US dollars for one hour."

"No, thank you, I brought my own with me."

"You Americans are cheap. Asian and Middle eastern men pay that".

GOODBYE HELISINKI!

I took a partner on a bus tour of Europe. The charter company was from Lichtenstein. Their bus drivers had to speak five languages. Whenever we stopped, the bus driver would be swamped by other tourist asking questions, knowing they could communicate with the driver.

We got into Lugano, Switzerland late. At check-in, the clerk told us to leave our luggage in the lobby and go to the dining room, they're holding it open for us. After our tour, we ate dinner and went to check –in.

We were told the hotel was over booked and needed two room reservations to volunteers to go to another location for the night. A single man, my partner, and I volunteered.

The hotel manager said, "Hurry, hurry, we have to rush you there. It was an old retirement home. They lock the doors at 10:30."

It had an old wooden creaky elevator. When we finally got in bed and pulled the covers up, they only came up about half way between our elbows and shoulders. If you pulled the covers up all the way, your feet stuck out from your knees down. We took the blanket and sheet off, placed the sheet on the bed with the top pulled up to the pillows. We tucked the blanket in the foot of the bed and pulled it up over the sheet as far as it would go. The sheet was all we had to keep the top part of our bodies warm. We had to hold each other to keep warm. It's not like we hadn't done that before. I mean, hold each other in bed.

SAS Flight Home

Freezing cold and the snow very deep, my partner thought the trip was a great Christmas present. The beverage service had no bourbon, only scotch. I asked the flight attendant if I could use my own bourbon.

"Yes, but don't let anyone see you."

Two couples were on the flight that that toured Moscow with us. One of the women came up to my seat and said, "They don't have any bourbon on board. We watched you hand out bottles of JD. You wouldn't have any left that I could buy?"

I asked, "Is it just the four of you?"

"Yes," was her reply.

"What's your seat number? I have to keep it out of sight."

I put eight bottles in the barf bag, walked back to her seat and gave them to her. She looked in the bag, motioned to her husband for money. I reached over, grabbing his arm. "It's on me, enjoy."

They thought I'd given them the world.

The flight attendant was taking dinner orders. The two choices were reindeer or salmon. Growing up on a farm in Iowa, we ate a lot of deer.

"I'll have a chunk of Rudolf. " I told the flight attendant.

There was a family with little kids sitting in front of me. They started screaming and crying. They thought I was going to eat Rudolf the Red-Nosed-Reindeer. For the remainder of the flight, I got mean, dirty looks from the kids.

Travel note: Big Mac in China $1.37, Hong Kong $1.27

As I traveled internationally, every place I went to I'd purchase a couple of wine glasses. When setting the table to entertain, I want a different wine glass at each place setting. The glasses are a great source of conversation. Also, if the conversation is boring, I look at a person taking sips of wine and my mind mentally opens two files, one of all the great women I've experienced and two of all the great vacations.

Back to the purpose of this, whatever you want to call it!

I've been very fortune to have a job that provided lodging and subsistence. This allowed me to budget $2,200.00 a month for laughs, shits, and giggles. Due to my wide variety of interest and what women exposed me to, I soon find myself dating several women at the same time. You cannot white-table cloth dine one woman and the next night with a different woman a beer and burger. I was able to concoct a spread sheet which helped spread the money around. I soon reached a point when money wasn't a consideration.

I always traveled alone. Fellow single guys were always asking to run with me. And I tell them, "NO! I travel alone." I don't want to have to look after someone when I get evolved. Many were the times I'd go into a place with live music and a dance floor asking women to dance. At the end of the song, I'd escort her to her seat, I'd go back to the edge of the dance floor, stand facing the crowd, hands wide, motioning for anyone woman to come on down.

If I was at a dance asking women to dance, the band announced a woman's choice, if I was not asked to dance, I'm history ladies. On to the next place!

HERPES

(TO SCREW OR NOT SCREW)

I met a gal at a Sadie Hawkins dance. We hit it off and had a great time. We talked about a wide verity subjects. After the Sadie thing was over, a band played good dance music. The Sadie thing ended early. The gal said, "Let's go to that motel down the street and have a drink. They have a fanatic 50s rock-and-roll band. After we have a drink or two and feel up to it, we can do a little R and R.

Rock and roll and motel – now, that got my attention! I'll stop at the desk on our way in and make a room reservation.

At the motel, I asked my gal, "Do you think we know enough about each other to be good mattressonime partners? Should I get a room?"

She said, "The answer is yes if whatever that word you used means sex. Get a room? No. I know bedding you would be fantastic, but I can't tonight."

Bedding? I'm thinking, never heard a talk like that. This gal got it together. So I told her, "Let's drink, dance, and then we can talk."

We were so good on the dance floor couples stopped dancing, stood on the edge and watched us.

The band took a break. She folded her hands on the table and looked me straight in the eye and said, "I have herpes. No matter how bad I'd like to spend the night with you, I have too much respect for you to infect you. My herpes was given to me by a friend I've known for a long."

Suddenly, that hard thing in my pants went soft.

She continued, "When we get back in your car I can give you head." I took her hands in mine and told her, "One sided sex gives me no pleasure. I only get my enjoyment when we both achieve fluffiness together."

"I'm the nursing coordinator. When my herpes is in remission, I'll have a doctor sign a note stating that. I'll call you and we'll plan a terrific weekend. How do you feel about naked hot tubbing?"

One day, she called.

"Hi Herpes," were my greetings. "I have a note. You plan Saturday's activities." She said.

"Okay, we will have brunch at ten, casual theatre performance at one, easy stroll after the theatre, then naked soak- n'- poke at four and dinner when hungry."

She replied, "Come by at 7:00a.m. so we can get the feel of each other, take a shower. Mine's big enough for two, and it'll take a long time drying each other."

"You can modify my plans anytime you want".

She enjoyed all the tools in my foreplay tool box. We had off-the-scale good times.

Must move on.

Of all the many sexual encounters I've had, I have never had one case of sexually transmitted disease!!

Every time I hear and see the word "herpes" it triggers a mental movie of Herpes and our times together.

REAL ESTATE SEX I

I was working at a remote location. After dinner, I walked into the cocktail lounge of the motel I was staying at. Nice atmosphere, soft lights, and slow dance music. I ordered my three fingers Knob Creek, two cubes and a splash. Looking around, I saw a late middle age lady sitting by herself. I watched her for a while. No one even came close to her. So I introduced myself.

"I'm up here on a job. Would you like to dance?"

I guess she was fifty. She was a very good dancer. When the music stopped, I walked her back to her table.

She said, "We're both here by ourselves. Sit here with me. I'm a real estate agent selling the new subdivision. I just got the office set up and the model open. I sit in an empty unit all day by myself. No traffic yet." And that was the beginning of my conversation with her. We had an enjoyable time dancing and visiting.

The band ended for the night.

I said, "I guess that means bed time," and went to get up.

She reached out touching my arm and said, "We're both here alone. We enjoy each other. Come and spend the night with me."

She was a little old fashion but game for anything except anal sex. During foreplay, if I did something my partner objected to, I promise I'd never go there again.

We spent the nights together for the week I was there. In our home towns, we lived about fifteen miles apart. We exchanged phone numbers and addresses.

The night before my job ended, I told her I'd be leaving town in the middle of the afternoon the next day.

She said, "Stop by the model on your way out of town."

So I did. When I entered the model, she got up from her desk and was all over me, kissing and feeling. She led me to an empty bedroom and started undressing. We laid down on the bare floor and had sex.

I called her when we were both back home and made date to meet her for a day in her hot tub. Sex in the water wasn't that enjoyable. I guess I'm a land lubber!

REAL ESTATE SEX II

A girl I was dating received an invitation to a wedding. We both knew the father and mother of the groom. After the wedding, we were socializing and dancing. My gal was off chatting with girlfriends. A lady I'd seen dancing with her husband, I'd guess fiftyish, came up to me, took my hand, pulled me close, and whispered, "I've been watching you. Let's dance."

On the dance floor, she pulled me close, rubbing against me. When the song ended, she turned sideways letting her hand feel my hard-on. I walked close behind her off the floor. Went to my chair, sat down, slid forward to get my lap under the table cloth.

My gal came back and said, "Let's dance."

I told her, "Let's wait a minute, I've been dancing".

The lady caught me again when my partner went off with a group to look at wedding gifts. On the dance floor holding me close, she said, "God, I want you now. After I felt you, I couldn't stand it. I searched around looking for a secluded place we could go."

While dancing, I learned she was a real estate agent but didn't have a place we could meet. I gave her my office number. She called and wanted to meet at a secluded bar. We sat in a darken booth. As soon as we sat down, she had my pants unzipped, playing with the stem end of my bladder.

"Keep doing that very long and I'll ejaculate."

Then she said, "Don't worry. I'll pretend I'm looking for something on the floor."

She did a great floor trick. I managed to finger her until she climaxed.

"Let's go to my office. We have a secure room that locks from the inside we use when taking private information." At the office, I took a folder from my desk, acted like we were reviewing information. I grabbed a tablet and went in the *locked room*. She took off her panties and sat on the end of the conference table. I laid her back, putting her legs over my shoulders. She grabbed the edges of the table and I inserted. It didn't take very long even though I'd just been sucked dry thirty minutes ago. After we were done, I gave her my handkerchief to put in her panties. I was very interesting as I watched her take a corner of the hanky, roll it in a tight twist, and inserted as much as she could, leaving the rest as a pad.

A week later, I received a package at the office. I opened it. It was my handkerchief. The note read, "I didn't wash it so you could have it for a remembrance in your trophy case."

I never talked to her again.

Sexcapade Timeline

(TRANSITIONING FROM ME PLAYING WITH IT TO HER EXPANDING IT INTO SOMETHING MUTUALLY SATISFYING)

I don't know if this is the correct place, this explanation of my explosion into the world of sex. Writing is tasking for me as I cannot spell and this God-damn spell check lacks the ability to understand what I'm saying. But I feel an early timeline would give the reader a better perspective of my rapid ascent into a sexually mature man.

- Graduated high school
- Left Iowa
- San Francisco
- Fellow employee gave me his pilot's license to drink with the coworkers
- Bought a Corvette
- Sex with a married woman in that Corvette
- Transferred to Hawaii, company shipped the Vette
- Traveled to four foreign countries
- Met a secretary on a trip to a foreign country
- She paid her own way to Hawaii to spend a month with me (Covered above in the INTERNATIONAL SEX section)
- A wife asked me to be her partner in joining wife swapping club
- Twenty-two years old, single, living in Hawaii, driving a Corvette, in a wife-swapping club!

MOM!
GUESS WHAT YOUR LITTLE BOY DID TODAY!

HAPPY 23rd FUCKING BIRTHDAY!
S F L (SINGLE LIFE FOREVER)
AND WE AINT EVEN GOT A GOOD START

ALMOST THREE-WAY-SEX I

NO BRASS RING

In the Pope meets Wild Indian section, where the neighbor man taught her how to enjoy anal sex, this is a new twist. She said, 'How do you feel about three-way sex?"

Stunned with my mind racing, I was picturing a man on each end of a woman. WOW! OFF THE SCALE!

She said, "I've been thinking about it for a long time." The neighbor man and I were talking about it but after you came along, I cut him off. He's so damn mad at me that we don't speak anymore and he wants kill you."

I told her, "Yes, let's do it. I want the ass end. The third would lay on the bed, you bent over, and do the mouth bit and I'd do the ass end. Do you have anyone in mind for the third?"

So we went prospecting for a third. It's not as easy as you think. You can't just walk up to someone and say, "I need a third for a three-way, want to join us?"

I got people asking, "What's your handicap?" And I'd tell them, "No, it's three-way sex. I got the ass end, you get the blow job. Are you in?"

No matter how hard we tried, we never found a third.

ALMOST THREE-WAY-SEX II

A very senior manager's wife and I were very friendly. She was a biker gal in her younger life, always making sure her tattoos were covered. She was always afraid her husband would find out about her past life. She, as well as all the managerial staff, knew about the women in my life. They just didn't know the extent of the sex stuff.

She said, "My husband shocked me last night. He asked me if I'd be willing to have three-way sex! As you know I'm still riding my Harley with a local club. He knows from my tattoos and old leathers I have, I ran with rough guys."

"Do you and your husband have anal sex?"

Her reply was, "No. I did when I was in the clubs as part of the biker ritual."

I asked, "Did you enjoy?"

"No! But if it would make my husband feel more macho, I'd do it for him. Even at his age, I just don't think he's mature enough to handle it."

So I told her, "When you think he's ready, I'll be the third."

She said, "I just knew you'd be willing. Have you ever been on a Harley?"

"No."

"Let's go for a ride if you don't mind a woman driver."

Ridding behind this fiftyish woman was a blast.

"You can raise your hands up a little higher."

"I didn't want to raise them too high," was my reply.

She took one of my hands and placed it on her breast. "Now you got your hand on my tit, I'll reach around and feel your crotch."

"Now we change hands, both tits need attention." She reached around to grasp my crotch.

"My God is that thing as big as it feels?" Laughing, she continued, "You don't have a sock in your pants, do you?"

"No, what you feel is what you get."

"I've got to see that CLUB. I know a very secluded place I like to ride you all by myself." She parked the bike and put the kick stand down. I swing sideways to get off. She stopped me. She unzipped my pants and it was instant road side lip service. I zipped up my pants. She led the way along a path to a spot out of sight of the road. She turned and was all over me. We laid down on our clothes. Going through my mental tool box of foreplays, as soon as I fingered her anus, she rose to her hands and knees.

I CLUBBED her. I placed one arm around her waist to hold her back against me and the other gently squeezing her nipples. When satisfied, we laid side by side until normal breathing returned. She turned, laying her head across my body, kissing, and rubbing my club all over her face.

We never did the three-way thing but we had many, many super mattresoname sessions. She truly liked it when I clubbed her in the ass.

The last words she spoke to me were, "Every time I have sex, I'll be thinking of you. I never imagined I'd enjoy being clubbed."

One last kiss and I took my club and left the field.

CAR SEX

At a dance, I noticed a gal who seemed out of place, just a little more upbeat, stylish, and nice looking. She kept watching the door as if waiting for someone. I went over to her table.

"I see you watching the door, cops coming to get you? Are you waiting for your girlfriend?"

"No, a guy," she replied.

"Are you and he an item?"

"No, just marking time until I find someone I want to be with."

"Well, I wouldn't want him to get the wrong impression when he walks in. I'll take a stool at the bar and work the crowd. There are lots of nice single gals in here."

At the bar, I ordered my standard, three fingers 100 proof Knob Creek, two cubs, and splash. Sipping t, surveying the prospects, a gal a couple stools down came up beside me.

"Dance with me and you don't even have to buy me a drink."

She was fair looking, a piss-poor dancer. I was glad when the music stopped. Getting her settled back on her stool, I motioned for the bartender.

"Give the gal a bottle of champagne, put it on my tab."

I walked to the back room out of her sight. Sure as hell, I don't want to get anchored down by her. Just in case, I kept looking at the door as if waiting for someone. It wasn't long before the first gal came up to me.

"I can't imagine anyone standing you up."

"No, I'm trying to give that barracuda at the bar the impression I'm waiting for someone so she won't approach me."

"I saw you buy her a bottle and vanished. Anyway, I guess my friend isn't going to show up, so I have two choices – go home or stay. Will you join me?"

"Sure. I wanted to do that the first time but you chased me off."

After a few dances, she said, "It's a great evening. Why don't you follow me home? I'll drop my car off and we can take a drive off along the coast."

I responded, "Follow the leader." I motioned toward the door.

We drove along the coast when I came to turn off where we could park and look over the ocean. We got out of the car and stood on a slight cliff watching the white caps. The breeze was a little chilly and she snuggled up close. I put my arms around her.

"I'm getting a little cold. I think we should sit in the car. In the car, I started the motor and turned the heater on. She raised the arms between the seats and slid close to me. The gentle caressing, kissing, touching, she encourage me to touch her body.

She spoke, "I think we should head home."

I cut over to the freeway and seventy-five miles an hour. She laid her head on my lap.

"Take a nap, we'll be home in a little while."

"Don't make it too soon."

With that, she unzipped my pants, finding the hole in my underwear, touching it.

"That feels pretty big."

"It's still soft."

"Let me get it out. I'll be the judge of the size."

"I know how big it is but you be the judge."

"Watch the road. I'll do the lip service. I think Long Tom, would be a good name, like a missile."

Even after she stopped the fluid flow, she still didn't want to call game over. She laid her face against it, feeling it. It didn't bother her that it's soft. I slowed as we approached her house.

"I'll put Tommy Boy to bed now." Back in place, she zipped my pants. I yelled when the hairs caught in the zipper. I started to get out to walk her to the door. She stopped me, gave me a long kiss, patted Tommy, "I left my go find me info in the door pocket. I want to see you soon. I can find my way to the door."

"I'll set here with the lights on until I see you're in."

A couple of days later, while reading the entertainment section, I saw an advertisement for the Ramona Pageant.

I called her, "The Ramona Pageant is on. Would you like to go?"

She said, "Sure, outdoors, the natural contour of the land, sitting Greek style, fun, fun, fun."

"I'll get tickets. The town is about fifty miles away, show starts at 2:00p.m. I'll pick you up at noon. We'll get something to eat at the theatre."

The performance was everything you could have hoped for. Gauchos on horseback, Indians screaming out of the hills and when it was over we were thoroughly entertained.

We were on the road in late afternoon. She said, "I'm going to lie down." She raised the seat arms and laid her head in my lap. As she lay there, I brushed her hair and face with my hand. Soon she started nuzzling my crouch with her head.

"I miss Tom." She said. "I think about us all the time. I want to relive that first date."

"We're too far from the ocean." I replied.

She rose up, unzipped my pants, located Long Tom and dug him out. Kissing him, the lip service begun. I slid my seat back as far as I could to give her more room. Like in the past, the trucks and pickups that could see us, buzzed around giving both side a look. As usual, I put my finger across my lips and shook my head telling them to be quite. Soon the well was dry. She laid her cheek against Tom and went to sleep. About thirty minutes later she spoke, "Let's stop at that cocktail lounge by my turn off. We can get in the back seat."

I said, "I don't know if I can get reloaded that soon."

"You just don't have confidence in me as a reloader."

I responded, "If you can, I'll let you pull the trigger."

It took longer than I thought reloading Tom.

I asked, "Trying to find the instructions? Do you have anything to lubricate it with? That usually helps".

She replied, "The barrels' bent a little, but I'm getting it straightened out. Ok, it's reloaded."

Then I instructed her, "Be really careful, it's a hair trigger. Keep your hand away from the end of the barrel. If the gun goes off it could blow your hand off."

Back seat entertainment was successful. We dressed good enough to swiftly get to the restroom before anyone notices us.

Seated, sipping our drinks, she said, "We're going to sit here talking, touching and dancing until Tom tells me we need to get in the back seat again. We did a lot of great slow dancing.

"You want another drink?"

"No," she said. "Tom doesn't like it when there's much drinking."

Dancing, holding me close she said, "I feel Tom getting restless. We need to get in the back seat and give him the attention he needs."

Let's figure this up. Thirty-five miles of oral sex and two back seat everything. It was a great production for twelve hours of work.

FACT: FOUR PERCENT OF THE WOMEN I DATED LIKED TO GIVE ORAL SEX WHILE I WAS DRIVING. I DON'T CARE IF IT WAS NIGHT OR DAY, FREEWAY OR ACROSS TOWN.

THE LANGUAGE I USE IS ACTUALLY THE WAY I TALK TO WOMEN. THEY ALL ENJOYED THE BACK-AND-FORTH JOKING, RACEY, ENGAGING STYLE. IF YOU CAN'T STAND THE HEAT, GET OUT OF MY BED!

MULTIPLE CLIMAXES I

I hadn't seen this gal for a while. When she accepted my re-get-acquainted offer, I told myself I need to make it a little special.

"Ok that's a date for Saturday. Can we have the whole day?"

"Sure," she said.

"First let's get together Thursday evening for a subway sandwich and a Starbucks."

We were sitting, eating our subway sandwich, I told her, "I want Saturday's date special for you". Here's a paper and pen. Make a list of everything you want to do in the time frame you set. I need to know in case I need to make arrangements."

We chatted while she wrote, pausing to think, "If I miss something can I still add to the list?"

I told her, "Anything can be added right up to the time I pick you up Saturday morning, unless I have to make arrangements."

"Finally, here's the list."

I gave the list a quick glance. It says 7:30- get up, coffee in bed.

"That won't work for me. I get up, get dressed, come to your house, and get back in bed."

She was laughing, "Your mind must be slowing down. If you stayed the night, wouldn't that make it easier?"

So I continued reading the list. Shower together, help each other dress.

"Can you still put panties on with your teeth? It always makes me laugh. Me laying on my back in bed, feet straight up in air, you getting my feet in the leg holes, pulling them down and that little extra thing you do when you stick your nose in the bed of roses, I get up on my hand and knees, feeling your nose between my buns as you pull the panties up over my butt, I lay down on back, you getting your second sniff of the roses as you work at getting the front panty band in your teeth, pulling the panties the rest of the way up.

Nodding, I said, "Yes, but I've modified it. It got too hard, too wobbling, standing up on the bed. Now you lay on your belly, feet bent upward at the knees".

I went on reading the list. At 9:30, champagne breakfast looking out over the ocean, walk by the bay, antique mall, house wares store, seafood lunch, go to my place, drinks and rest, get dressed, fish n" chips at bagpiper place, theatre, toad in the hole after the theatre, home, night cap, bed.

"OK Saturday's date is settled. Now, let's get you home. You need rest for work tomorrow."

She said, "No! I'm going to find out tonight if you're as good as I remember before I waste my Saturday."

"Well, don't get so excited that you start you period and waste my Saturday," was my reply.

"Who cares? I haven't forgotten the three-two game."

At work, the phone rings. "It's me. You're qualified for Saturday."

"Good, I won't be trapped on Saturday with Rosie Palm and her five sisters."

I arrived at her house Friday late evening carrying take out. Eat, drink, movie, bed. Her fragrance engulfing, body was so soft. We did the physical relaxing technique. It made me so soft and restful. I fell asleep curled up smelling my fingers.

Saturday morning, I jokingly went down her list barking out each item off at the proper time like a drill sergeant.

The day and evening was so much fun as we checked off each item. Getting up from the table after finishing the toad in the hole, I checked off the second to the last item, showing her the only thing on the list, HOME.

We fixed a drink and headed for the bedroom. We were so relaxed and contented. The last sip, lights out, curled together, and we were soon sound asleep. Little did I know that the next day would add a new domination to my sex knowledge.

Sunday brought a late morning awakening. The room seemed electrifying. Are bodies responded to each other like drawn by a magnet. With her help guiding the way, penetration was effortless. We were both so ready, almost instantaneously, we reached satisfaction. No jerking, no verbalization, just holding each other tight in loving embrace. We lay relaxed.

She said, "I'll use this one, you use the guest and get the coffee. You know how I like it."

Back in bed, moving next to each other, gently letting hands play over bodies, casually rising to sip coffee. Brushing my hand across her nipples, her body gave jerking motions.

"Boy, I never felt that climax coming," she said.

My hands played over a sensitive point on her body and again a jerking motion, "What are you doing to me? That's another climax."

"It must be the room. The air seems different," I said.

"I need to get up. I can't believe what's happening to me."

So I asked, "Is your body in distress?"

"No. I feel good, kind of out of my body," she said.

After moving around and another cup of coffee, she said, "Let's get back in bed, it feels so right being next to you".

She kicked the covers off, lying on her stomach. I started rubbing her back, kissing her down her buttocks. There was another jerking, another climax. She hardly reacted and didn't say a word. I kept kissing her down the buttocks.

She cocked one leg to where I could feel the hair of the pleasure pit with my tongue. And another jerking climax. I kept kissing the back of her leg and reached the inside of her tight, another climax. Then, kissing the back of her knee there was another climax. She turned over on her back. After the fourth climax, I started keeping count.

She said, "I want to feel you inside me."

I told her, "I've been so blown away with your body's responses, having sex never entered my mind."

"I can't do it with a flap."

"Let me use my lips and speak to it."

Her magic breath miraculously breathed life into the flap inflating to a pole. With her helping hands entrance into the ARCH de PLESURE was successful. Working together, the deposit was made.

Honest truth. When I counted her twelfth climax, I looked at the clock. It was 3:00 pm.

"It's three o'clock? Think we should get vertical?" I asked.

"I guess. I feel like a limp rag. Take a shower with me. I may need you to hold me until I regain my senses".

"You climaxed twelve times, but who's counting. My thumb and finger are numb. I may lose the use of them," I jokingly replied.

We went out for a combination of breakfast, lunch, and dinner.

I sit her in bewilderment. Where do these strong, high-energy, intelligent women come from? What was it that these women took me into their lives.

NOW, IF YOU THINK TWELVE CLIMAXS WAS UNBELIVABLE? HANG ON TO YOUR ASS. BECAUSE YOU AIN'T GONNA BELIEVE WHAT'S NEXT!!!

MULTIPLE CLIMAXES II

Remember POPE meets Mensa section from earlier in this writing? The gal with the scar on her face, her husband smashed a bowel into it? She took me to college with her?

I thought Mensa could use some kindness. When I read in the paper that Richard Burton and Camelot were coming to town, I bought two tickets for the best seats in the theatre.

I called her up, "Mensa! This is Jim Pope, remember me?"

"Oh, Jim! It's good to hear your voice," was the reply on the other end.

So I continued, "Burton is coming to town with Camelot. If I sent you a first-class ticket, will you fly in and go with me?"

I picked Mensa up at the airport.

I told Mensa, "The first thing we're doing is go shopping. Our tickets are for dress circle. We'll get you decked out for the theatre."

She was absolutely beautiful.

"Let's go home, change into play clothes, and attack the town."

Late evening, curled up on the double recliner sipping drinks, and reminiscing.

Mensa said, "The professor told me he has done research and has incorporated a lot of the things you told his class into his curriculum."

Burton and Camelot was fantastic. We dropped in for some fish n' chips, and a bagpiper music. When we got home I asked, "Do you want a drink to relax?"

She pulled me to her, full mouth kisses. "I just want us to go to bed."

After short foreplay, she said, "I want to feel you in me, you know, where I get most pleasure."

She grabbed a pillow and upon anal entry, she had the pillow pulled over her face and letting out muffled screams. Her violent jerking caused my gun to go off. We got up, washed, and got back in bed.

In the morning when I woke up, I softly stroked her, the room became electrifying, and she came alive.

"Sex in the morning with you, I've been living with that memory."

I then gently brushed her arm. The jerking motion signaled climax. I touched her belly, climax. I touched her nipples, climax. I brushed her face, climax. I fingered the center cut, climax. Slight finger insertion, she climaxed. I counted seventeen climaxes. I got on top for vaginal sex, we both reached satisfaction at the same time. Eighteen climaxes in a row.

IF YOU THINK EIGHTEEN CLAIMAXES IS UNBELIEVABLE, THIS WILL KNOCK YOU RIGHT ON YOUR ASS! AND IT'S GOD DAMN TRUE!

MULTIPLE CLIMAXES III

I met a very upbeat gal, full of energy. We dated and mattressoname a few times. She was also open to anything sex wise. I used the predate technique of Thursday planning "her Saturday" using the same format used in MC I and MC II.

Sunday morning, the old electrifying air filled the room. Climax, climax, climax and more climaxes. We stayed in bed all day. When I called a stop to the game, my hand was getting numb.

TWENTY-FOUR CLIMAXES!!!! OK, you Peter stickers, top that!!

Nun-Sense

Now this almost made a church believer out of me. I noticed a woman in our complex I had not seen before. I asked some of the gals I worked with about her. When I learned she is new, I felt it was my duty to approach and welcome her. I guessed her to be in her late forties, rather attractive, modern hair style, and nice figure. She was very outgoing. I made it a point to joke and chat with her. She thought my name being Pope was very funny. She asked me about my religious philosophy. I told her on Sunday mornings I listened to Western church music on TV. During our conversations, she told me she was an ex-nun. She wanted to get into politics which was not allowed, so she kicked the habit. She also told me about her interests - church, art, theatre, antiques, and junking.

As I enjoyed those things, except the churchy stuff, I asked if I could go along with her to culture events. As I tried to get close to her, she kept her distance. After an early date, she asked me in. After offering, a drink she sat apart from me. Although the conversation was very interesting, I was hoping for a little something more.

"Our church is having a bazaar Saturday. Come by I'd like you to meet my priest. I know you'll like him."

Saturday came, "Father I'd like you to meet Jim Pope."

"Oh, thank you lord, the POPE has arrived. When word get spread around the POPE is here our attendance will EXPLODE," The priest declared.

"Father, I'm qualified to hold commune on airplanes with a jug of RIPPLE and a bag of crotons and it does get me closer to heaven."

"We use a better grade of grapes in our church wine," he said.

"I saw this movie *Grapes of Wrath*. I hope your grapes don't come from the same vineyard."

"Why don't you come to church with *the nun*? We'll give you a taste of our wine and you be the judge."

"I'll pass father." I declined his invitation and continued, "I'll stay loyal to my TV Cowboy church."

I really enjoyed joking with the priest and attended other church functions with *the nun*.

I told the priest, "Father, if you ever need a backup, pencil me in." How could you not like a guy like that?

Evening, we went to her house after the theatre. I flopped down on the couch, telling myself, if nothing happens, I'm outta here. She lay down on the couch, on her belly, feet in my lap. I told myself I'm not going to sit looking at her ass if I have the equipment to stick something in it.

My own words came floating across my mind, MAKE IT HAPPEN, LET IT HAPPEN, WHAT THE FUCKS HAPPENING!

I started rubbing her feet. The more I gently massaged her feet, the more contented her verbalizations were. My god! She's going to sleep! I brought one of her feet up to my mouth and started nibbling on her toes.

"What are you doing?"

I answered, "Are you enjoying it?"

"Oh yes. Never experienced anything like that."

I started gently sucking on her toes. What?! I noticed some positive response so I began full sucking on her toes, rubbing her ankles. She settled from thrashing the legs. Hey, we're getting somewhere, so I thought. Moving my hand up to the calf and leaning over, kissing the back of her knees, things got more intense. Gently massaging, pushing my hand further up on the inside of her thigh, she spread her legs apart. Kissing the inside of her thigh, pushing my hand up, fingers touching her panties, she jerked to her feet, pulled me up and dragged me to the bedroom.

She did not want foreplay. No tit sucking, no kissing, nothing stuck in her ass. Straight vaginal intercourse! She cleared the brush covering the ARCH entrance, holding the lips apart with two fingers and guiding the insertion with the other hand. When I'd given all I had to give, she kept holding me tight. Finally relaxed, she released me. I withdrew, laid side by side, recovering.

WHAT HAPPENED NEXT WAS THE BEST FREE SIDE SHOW I EVER ATTENDED.

Thirty minutes after we finished our mattressoname session, I watch as she inserted her middle finger in the Arch De Pleasure. Pulling out the sperm-coated gummy finger, she held the lips apart with two fingers and massaged her clitoris with the gummy finger. Her body response was

more thrashing than with normal vaginal satisfaction. I was waiting for her to lick her finger, she never did. In fact, she wiped it on my chest hair.

"Are you shocked?"

"I believe everyone should be satisfied."

But from then on, I always watched out for sticky fingers!

We were together only a couple more times as she got a job with the educational department of the US government.

I never once kissed her or nuzzled her nipples!!

Dear Mom,
Guess what your little boy saw today!?

PIANO BAR SEX I

Isn't that a TV station?

I entered a hotel I had never been to before. Entering the piano bar, I recognized the piano player. I walked up to the piano bar.

"Ruddy Reed! You, in person."

I turned to the people sitting and standing around the piano.

"Do you know who this is?" pointing to Buddy." They all looked at me like saying, "You stupid ass."

"That's Regis Philbin's TV piano player."

"Sit down, shut up POPE!" I told myself.

I sat down on a stool next to little over weight gal. She had great looks and personality. Everyone was having a great time listening, talking, and singing. After a couple of hours, the gal leaned over, "Will you go home with me?"

In bed, she wanted everything sex had to offer, starting with getting on top, knees on each side of my ears. She passed the sniff test.

"If I stick my tongue in that ARCH, between those inviting lips, it won't bite me, will it?"

"It's very tame. Try it, you'll like it." We did all three holes.

Next morning when I dropped her off at her at her house after we had breakfast, she was getting out of the car when she handed me her card. "Monday afternoon around 4:30 come by my office."

I had had trouble finding her office. She was a freight forwarder in a small one-person store front office, in the industrial part of the city.

She was at her desk when I walked in. She pulled out the work board from one side of her desk. Padding it, she said, "Here I have your bed ready."

I sat down on the work board, back to the window. No fan fair, she unzipped my pants, pulled out the stem end of my bladder, and when she got it hard she performed lip service. Ejaculation completed, she licked the stick clean. I got up and zipped my pants. She was saying as I walked out the door, "I liked that flavor POPEcycle."

I never saw her again.

PIANO BAR SEX II

There's nothing exciting. She did not move in bed. Get in bed, she got it hard, she cleared the hair covering the ARCH, help insert, moved her head back and forth when she climaxed. I got up and left. Just excited the shit out of me!

PIANO BAR SEX III

I walked into a piano bar and sat down beside a woman, drank and sang. She leaned over saying, "I don't want to stay her any longer."

I followed her to her place. No kissing, no foreplay (my foreplay tools are getting rusty), undressed, and she cleared the ARCH opening. I did learn it is common thing for women to do because women get haircuts when the male inters. So now it's a side cut, on the center cut. Maybe I should just cut out. This sex stuff is getting so confusing. Now, this gal must have been in her late fifties. She cried, moving her head back and forth the whole time it was inserted and she was motionless. I asked her if I was hurting her. She just held me tighter. I pulled the covers up over her, left her curled up crying. I locked the door on my way out.

Not all's lost. I did get to liking piano music.

Partner and I were in bed, just after the big explosion. Partner got out of bed and went to the bathroom to do a little cleaning and dusting. She came out carrying the waste basket.

"Your bathroom stinks. If you're going to have guests that are having their period, empty waste basket after they leave." She set the basket outside the back door.

In bed with a partner about ready for the big explosion, I hear the distant *click, click, click* getting louder coming up the sidewalk. I froze, telling my partner, "It'll go away." Then *tap, tap, tap,* on the window.

"Jim, Jim. I saw your Corvette in the driveway. Are you home and just going to bed early?"

My partner couldn't stop giggling.

Tap, Tap, tap. Pause. *Click, click, click,* fading.

My partner commented, "Oh, now that's funny. Now, we have to start all over again. Jim, I don't like these kinds of redos."

I made plans to take a partner for a long flyaway weekend. I was out with this gal for the evening for fish n' chips, darts, and drinks. I made up a fruit tray and placed it in the fridge for later when we came home to consume the contract. When we got home, we settled in the record room to listen to soft mood music and a night cap. I went to the kitchen for the fruit try and noticed the back door glass was broken and pieces of glass were all over the floor. I decided to clean it up and see if anything is missing. I got the fruit tray and returned to the record room for food and cozening before going to the bedroom for the contract signing. I picked up the dishes and entered the kitchen. The pantry door opened and out stepped a partner that's in the mattressoname mix. (I hate these God-damned red-lining computers). I understand the red line on the Vette. Why can't they make a computer like that?

Back to my story, I said to my partner, "Hey, what are you doing here?"

"Followed you and then came back here and broke in. I saw the airplane tickets. I thought we were an item."

I told her, "Get out! Get out!"

She answered, "No, I want to know why I'm not good enough to be taken on a trip?"

And an all-out brawl started. Fighting, rolling on the floor. My partner who I was going to take to bed was standing in the doorway leaning against the jam with her arms folded and laughing.

Finally, I was able to sit on her back and called 911. She's a little drunk. The police came. My partner-in-waiting, laughing all the time, let them in. She could hardly stop laughing long enough to tell the police what was going on. The Police got her up and cuffed her.

The Police said, "We'll hold her for four hours. We'll let her go when she's sober."

The partner-in-waiting helped me clean up the broken glass and tacking cardboard over the window, laughing almost uncontrollable. Now we're sitting on the kitchen floor leaning up against the cabinets. We're both giddy.

"That was the best floor shows I've ever seen."

"Shall we wait to sign the contract in the morning?" I asked.

"No. I'll blow you off, that'll cool you down."

I responded, "I think if I get a breathing aid I'll recover."

"They say if you breathe into a sack it will help. I don't have a sack but I've got something in my pants that might work."

Teasingly I said, "That's better. I like a sack that smells like roses. Let's get to bed so I can lie down and start the recovery process."

I got in bed, laid on my back, "Here, put the bouquet here," and I patted my face. "Oh, that smells so good. I could lie like this all night."

"I'm feeling left out. My clitoris is itching, wiggle your nose."

I looked at the clock, it's been four hours.

I said to my partner, "It's been fours. I need to take you home and get the jail bird. She's really a very nice girl".

Partner commented, "Now that's what I call fuckin' fast."

I picked up the jail bird. Got her something to eat and dropped off at her car. I went home, dropped in bed. The phone rang.

"Who in the hell's calling at this hour?"

"It's the flower vendor. It's three-thirty in the afternoon. I need to check that rose contract I signed. We got so engrossed in that wrestling match I just kind of skimmed over it. Be over in a few or do I need a reservation? I'll bring something you like and something to eat."

It's that meal sweeping the country call ON-and-OFF CLOTHES meal with do it yourself desert.
JUST ANOTHER DAY IN PARADISE!!!

WHAT! SINGLE IN A WIFE SWAPPING CLUB!

A DIFFERENT TIME A DIFFERENT PLACE

Once again, my Corvette leads the way. It's the best sex provider and helper I ever had. THANK YOU, GM, for not tossing it in the recycle bin in 1958.

My friend lived in the end unit of a four-unit condo. Knowing he didn't have much money, I'd often treat him and his wife to white table cloth dinning. She loved sitting on his lap, booming around in the Vette. It had the 283 with cam, 2 -4's, 4 on the floor. It was a screamer. I was a master speed shifter. Laying rubber in 1,2,3. The wife would howler with excitement as I floored it, not letting up until I hit fourth.

BACK TO WIFE SWAPPING: Whenever I would go over to visit my friend and his wife, the married neighbor gal that lived in the unit on the other end, would always come out to look at the Vette and speak to me.

One day, she said, "Before you leave knock on my door."

"Would like to go to a party with me tonight?"

I replied, "Sounds like fun".

Then she continued, "This is a different kind of house party. Only certain couples are allowed.

My husband doesn't like these parties. The company he works for works operates 24/7. On party nights, he will cover a job for a two for one. Meaning, he'll cover once for two covers in return."

So I picked her up, stopped to get a case of wine as a hostess gift. When we arrived, there were several couples present.

After a short social gathering, the hostess announced, "All men to the record room."

One woman objected, pointing at me "I'm not comfortable, he's not married."

The gal I came with said, "He's on trial. We'll be together. You'll find out with the morning report."

All of the men entered the record room, the hostess closed. Soon, she opened the door yelling," *COME AND GET IT!*"

The men shot out of the room, running to a pile of shoes on the floor. Each grabbing a shoe, ran to the women, and matching up the shoes. As soon as they found the mate, out the door they went. Three minutes and the place were empty.

The gal said, "You got me until 11:30 that's when my husband gets home."

I parked in front of her unit. "No, not here. Over there by those empty units.

After parking, she asked me, " Have you ever had sex in this car?"

"Yeah, the Vette's not a virgin," was my reply.

As always, it's hard in a Vette to get inserted into the sperm catcher. Surprise!

I asked her, "Your center cut is shaved. Did you have an operation? It'll pass the smell test with just a damp cloth and you don't get lip cuts."

Is this getting complicated or what? "I see, you get lip cuts on the center cut. With a little work, I think it could be a great song. Help me out here. Let's see, try this"

"Lip cuts on the center cut, teeth marks on the pleasure pole, brush covering the pleasure hole.

Hey, I think we got a hit song going."

By now we're laughing so hard. "OK, down to business." I instructed here, "Get the pants unzipped, and get your mouth involved. I know, it's hard to laugh with your mouth full."

"It's better this way. If we get serious, we'll think we're in love."

Foot prints on the inside of the windshield. Think anybody will notice?

We got serious and had the best no-bed sex. It was a thrill for her. This is my second sex in the Vette rodeo. That makes me A VETERAN!

I asked her, "How often do you hold these parties?"

"Once a month."

"How many couples are there?"

"Fourteen. Because of periods, the meeting numbers vary. Can I have your phone number? I'll turn it in to the club president."

"You mean I'll get a call from the president? I feel important."

"No," she said. "The day after each party, we have to give the president a report on our night's connection. When I tell the president about my SEX in the VETTE and the song you wrote, Hair Cut on the Center Cut, Teeth Marks on the Holly Pole, while She Played with My Lip Stick as you called it, she'll die. Gals will be waiting in line by the Corvette."

"Can you have sex with club women outside club parties?"

"Oh yes. These women are starved for new partners."

I attended two more parties, always leaving with a different wife. The big talk at the parties was that the company would be moving out of state. My company sent me out of country for three months. When I got back, there was a letter in my box from the gal who introduced me to the wife-swapping club telling me the company moved too. "Club still together. Stop by if you are in the area."

I sat down and ran the numbers. Eleven first timers, eight repeats in the Vetteteotel. Nineteen plus the one right after I purchased the Vette. Three more times and it would match my age. My single friends knew that I was doing a lot of sex in the Vette and were always asking if they could go with me when bar hopping.

I always turned them down saying, "I always run by myself. The guys would come by the Vette, stick their head in, sniff, and say, "Still parking by the dumpster at the fish market," laugh, and walk away.

DANCE FOOL, DANCE

I went into a ballroom I had never been in before. I stood back by the wall surveying the territory. As I watched, one gal really had it together on the dance floor. Her partner couldn't keep up with her, missing steps, and lagging behind. I watch when the music stopped to see where she sat. But she walked over to a group and mingled. I thought that's odd. The band played a couple more songs and she never went to the dance floor.

Now, something's wrong. I walked over, approached her.

"You're such a good dancer, why are you letting all this good music go to waste?"

"These are some of my students. I work at Arthur Murray's Dance Studio. I'm trying to expose them to the real world of social dancing."

So I introduced myself, "I'm Jim Pope. I wouldn't mind you dragging me around the floor. I'll try to keep up."

On the dance floor, we were in perfect lock step. It didn't make any difference what type of music was played, we were in locked step.

Off the dance floor, she said to her students, "This is Jim Pope. With just a little more practice you can be just like us."

"Where did you learn to dance?"

I told her and her students about my sisters and I learning steps in front of the TV during Lawrence Welk's TV show and a lot of fun dancing doing the polishing. When I saw a person doing something new to me, I'd ask to be shown the steps. Everyone is eager to show someone how much smarter they are than the other person. I got so many, many very good free lessons. The band started playing. I asked one of her older female students to dance.

She was hesitant and drew back, I told her, "It's my job to make you look like the best dancer on the floor. If we're dancing and you are having trouble, we go to the edge of the floor and very slowly walk through the steps. You'll earn the respect of everyone here for you. Understanding your short falls and doing something to correct. As couples danced by, I'd say to them, "Isn't she doing great?"

When we left the floor, she was all smiles and bubbly.

Instructor said, "It is so nice to go to a dance and find someone so polished. Come by the studio tomorrow evening, I want to introduce you to my manager."

When I entered the studio, some of the students who were at the dance the night before came running up to me. The student I asked to dance was all smiles. The music was playing. I took her out on the floor did our stuff.

"Did you feel how strong his lead is?" Instructed asked.

The student nodded yes.

Instructor continued, "You couldn't have made a mistake if you wanted to."

Then she introduced me to her manager, "Jim this is the manager, Manager, this is Jim Pope."

"Instructor told me about you teaching on a real dance floor. Thank you. The students have been telling me all about it. Frankly it was as if you gave them a shot of confidence," Manager said.

The instructor and I went out a couple of time dancing. Then one day, I got a call from her.

"Can you come to the studio tomorrow? The manager wants to talk to you."

Instructor and I were in the manager's office.

"I think we can help each other. Problem I have is that we have students that are slow learners and we must re-teach them, costing us money. Now, Instructor, you tell what we can do for him," Manager said.

"There is a West Coast regional dance contest in two months at Berkley. The winner goes to Las Vegas for the Western regional contest. We think you and I have a good shot at winning both contests. The manager has a sort of inside knowledge that will enhance our chances. You reteach our slow learners, the manager will work with us prepping for the contests," The instructor said, "Sounds like a deal to me."

The instructor and I did extra work at home. But we found out bed dancing was more fun. We did win the regional contest. A couple of days later, the company owner told me I'd be leaving for overseas in a couple of weeks.

Just another person having no luck with Vegas.

OFFICE SEX, MINE I

(Two-Fer Sounds better)

I stopped by a club where I played with the band whenever they needed a base player. I went up to the stage, waved to the guys, and retreated to the back of the room. I noticed two gals I'd seen before sitting together. *Lezzies*, I thought, "To each his own."

I walked over to their table. "You two an item?"

Both said, "No. Just friends that like to get out together."

"Without your husband's?" I added.

"No, we haven't had husbands for years. Husbands are too much trouble."

Our conversation continued, "I've seen you in here when I've fill in with the band."

"Yes, we've seen you, never had a chance to meet you. I'm a nurse," said the first gal.

The other one spoke up, "I work in admin at the same hospital."

Addressing both, I said, "That's some good dance music, either one of you, that's as far as I got." The nurse jumped up, grabbed my hand and headed for the dance floor. We had fun on the floor, slow music and bodies touching.

"Your body feels like it could do a pretty good job elsewhere."

Nodding yes with my head against hers, "Yaw, been there, done that."

"But not with me you haven't. From what I'm feeling, I'm ready for it anytime."

The song ended and I walked her back to the table. Ordered a round of drinks, put it on my tab. The music started up. I asked the second gal, "Partner, like to dance?"

On the floor, she danced just like the nurse. "Boy you too dance alike."

"I'm on a mission. Nurse told me to dance close and see if I get the same feeling and BOY do I."

She pulled me closer to her, sliding her hand down between us. Feeling the stem end of my bladder, rubbing up and down, she relaxed her hold, stepping back she turned us sideways so we could see the nurse. With one arm around my neck, she raised the other arm, holding her index fingers about a foot apart. The nurse made big eye, nodding yes.

The music stopped. Partner said, "Mission accomplished."

We were back at the table, sitting while the band changed instruments, sipping drinks, talking small talk.

"If you two would like a little time for yourselves, I can go to the bar."

Nurse said, "No, we've got plans for you we need to run past you."

"OK," I said. "You tell me your plans, and I'll tell you mine."

"We both want to take you to bed. We're just trying to decide who should go first."

"That's a no brainer. The nurse should go first to inspect the facilities."

Nurse said, "Yes, it's a no brainer."

"Partner, we just have to decide when the best time is. Maybe you should tell us."

"My office is four blocks down the street. It's got a very comfortable conference table. I'll slip out now, Nurse, you wait until it isn't obvious and I'll be waiting."

Surprise! It was a unanimous vote. "The yeses win."

I finished my drink, stood up, and in a louder voice said, "Well, it's been nice visiting with you, but I've got to leave the party."

I walked out, got in my car, and pulled as close to the door as I could. Nurse came out, got in the car and to my office we went.

The offices security lights were a dim glow. In the conference room, stripped from the waist down, throwing our clothes over the chairs. We played "you play with mine, I'll play with yours" while standing. Seeing me naked, she said "Partner wasn't lying."

She rolled up on the conference table. I rap my knuckles on the table, "Ok, let's bring this meeting to order." I grabbed her legs pulling her to the edge of the table. When her butt got to the edge, I put her legs over my shoulders. The table was just the right height.

Laughing, she said, "Another case of getting screwed by management."

"That's not fair. I'm giving you a raise as we speak."

She responded, "I have never gotten a raise this big before."

Getting dressed, nurse said, "I have every Wednesday off. I could use something stiff to wake me up. Is that something possible?"

"What time," was my only response.

"Seven in the morning."

"You'll have to get me ready when you get to my condo."

"I can do that."

"Keep this between us. I don't know yet about partner."

In the car, I said to her, "I'll drop you off. You can tell your friend how it went. I'll wait fifteen minutes. If partner comes out we'll repeat the process."

Partner exited the building, entering the car. "Nurse said it was a very interesting meeting."

She unzipped my pants, "I want to get a feel of what I'm getting into. Hurry, I can't wait!"

The second session was a little different. She wanted to stand, bending over holding on to the edge of the table. She used one hand doing the hair clearing routine and two fingers for the parting. It was a successful vaginal rear entry.

"Do enjoy anal sex?" I asked.

"It's Ok, but I like it the way we did it better. My ex and I would fall asleep in the spoon position with him inserted from behind. It's hard to break old habits."

I got together with her only one more time. Nurse and I did a lot of seven am meetings.

REMEMBER NURSE FROM OFFICE SEX I?

SHE'LL BE MAKING A RETURN APPERANCE TO "STEPPING STONES" IN A MAJOR ROLL ALONG WITH WILD INDIAN IN A MINOR ROLL IN THE FINAL EPISODE OF "STEPPING STONES," COMING UP NEXT IN THIS EARTH-SHAKING DRAMA

TRIFECTA!

(Better known as 3-Fer)

Insert my Trifecta flyer here
(No, this is not about horses.)

A little history before sex. Isn't that the way it's always been, study before play?

In high school, I fell in love with a classmate. She was smart, athletic, musician, hard working farm girl. I was just the opposite. At age fifteen when my father died in my arms, I replaced him as janitor of the Macedonia, Iowa, Consolidated School House, supporting my mother and little sister. At the end of the ninth grade, the school board asked me to stay on as janitor. I told them that I would be closing the school at the end of the school year and my family will move back to our home town of Avoca.

I took a job as a hired man on a farm in Neola, Iowa for John and Vonda Koch. The job lasted for four years when I left to get my life started.

OK, enough of this digging in the dirt! Let's create some dirt!!!

One more thing, in my novel *Trifecta*, Julia was the love of my life that I married.

During high school, she would only date me when she didn't have a better offer. I wasn't good enough for her. I had a full-time farming job. I was one of the two in our class that had their own car and the only that had a checking account.

Her mother really liked me. Julia took a job in Omaha at a private company. All the single gals in the office were after the owner's son. Julia played the sex card insuring her of marrying him. He married someone else.

To cut to the chase: My novel **Post Hole Digger** is the story of my life from first memory to joining the navy and entering the submarine force.

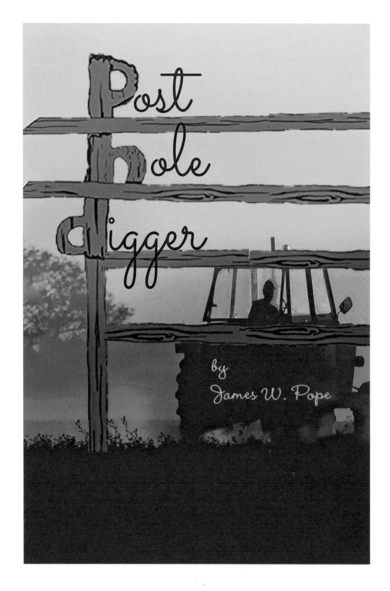

Post hole digger

by

James W. Pope

My novel Trifecta is a mix of actual experiences and my creative genius.

At the age twenty-seven, I married my high school sweetheart, even though she rejected me and my proposal, knowing I'd never be anything but a farmer. Her mother liked me from the first time I met her mom and dad. At that time, I was working on the farm as a hired man. Her dad and I got along very good.

We could discuss every aspect of farming on the level as if farm owner to owner. Her mother just couldn't do enough trying to get her daughter to see me in a better light. Her mom and I became very close.

She had to move from Iowa to San Diego.

She did not like San Diego or California. Soon after the marriage, she began to distance herself. I thought she was just depressed. I got her involved with the Red Cross swimming program. She became a very good swimmer earning the fifty-mile patch. She had a beautiful voice. We put together a country western band. She and our lead singer shared the singing duties. I still miss her singing the Lord's Prayer. I got her involved in an international women's singing group. We took up golf, became the club doubles champs. She had a little spine organ which she out grew. I bought her the biggest organ that could be placed in a house. We sponsored a women's softball team, which she played on. Our team was a city champ. She played trumpet in the high school band, played taps and echo taps at military funerals. I paid cash for a nice four-bedroom house in the Clermont section of San Diego. Sound like a real power couple. Looks can be deceiving.

When her folks came to San Diego, we had a blast. Took them to Los Angeles to the Palladium where Lawrence Welk's TV show was broadcasting from. I knew Welk had played at our local dance hall in Avoca, Iowa and my mother and father in-law had danced to his music. When the orchestra took a break, Lawrence stayed on stage with anyone that wanted to talk to him. I kept urging my wife's mom and dad to go up and talk to him. They were too shy. I kept urging them. Finally, I got up and said, "You'll never have another chance to talk to him. He'll be delighted to talk to someone that danced to his music in Avoca, Iowa!" They both slowly got up and the closer we got to the stage they walked happily, upbeat, to the stage. When we had a chance I said, "Mr. Welk, this is my mother and father-in-law, Norris and Verna Yeager from Avoca, Iowa, and they tell me they've danced to your music."

Lawrence's face broke into a big smile, "Oh yes. We played at Avoca, many times."

They started talking. I left and went back to my seat. When they came back from the stage they were floating on air. We took them to TJ. I told Verna, "I think you can get a job at one of these clubs. She and I always laughed and joked all the time.

I said to my FIL, "Let's take run down to the Body Shop."

MIL said, "Your wife and I will go shopping."

The Body Shop is a topless titty bar. My FIL is a deacon in the church but not a prude. He can tell some pretty raunchy jokes. I knew some of my fellow employees would be there for lunch. FIL had a great time watching the tits flop and looking at the cracks of asses. A few days later, the four of us were driving around and I purposely drove by the Body Shop. Huge vertical lighted sign and big pictures in the windows of skimpy-dressed women.

I stopped, "Here's the Body Shop where we were."

My MIL saw it, embarrassed.

Laughing, she gave me slap across the back of the head. "We had to go in there to make sure the tits were still flopping." And I was rewarded with another slap from MIL.

My wife had a daughter from her previous marriage. She was pregnant with our daughter. My MIL wanted to come out when the baby was due to help wife. One day, wife said to me, "Mom's been trapped in this house. Take her out for dinner this evening, she deserves it."

IN MY NOVEL, "TRIFECTA", YOU CAN READ EXACTLY HOW BUDDY REED, REGIS PHILBIN'S PIANO PLAYER AND CHRISTPHOR PLUMMER WERE RESOPNSIBLE FOR MY MOTHER-IN-LAW AND I HAVING OUR FIRST INTERCOURSE. SEXUAL RELATIONSHIP LASTED FOR THIRTEEN YEARS.

I went online to both Regis and Christopher's website informing them I was using this in my Trifecta novel. When no response, I wrote both a letter. Still no response.

I wrote Archie Panjabi a letter and sent her a copy of Trifecta, asking if she would be interested in attaching her name for the part of Julia if it becomes a movie. I mailed it to her agent. I'm waiting for a reply.

Within a year after our marriage I started noticing flaws in her. Very seldom was I able to get her sexually aroused. Now, you've read about all my sexual experiences and you can't get your wife aroused? I'm telling myself, what's wrong with this picture. The realization came when the high school had to discipline the female PE teacher for making girls show their protection as proof of period, for missing PE class. We had three lesbians on our softball team, the PE teacher was one of them. There were lesbians in the singing group. She and "some" of the softball girls are getting together for drinks. The PE teacher was always in the click. So, I suspected the same thing was happening with the singing group.

We had money to do anything we wanted to do. LA theatre, Disney Land. I cried when I sold my Corvette because it wasn't a family car. All that was left was memories of all the sex I had in that car. I purchased a Morgan. It was sports car with a back SEAT. I purchased Cadillac so she had something to drive her friends around in.

I was smoking at the time we were married. Living alone I didn't realize just how dirty the habit was. I had a carton of cigarettes at home, in the glove compartment of my car, a carton at work and I carried three different packs on me. Every time there was something that evolved money she would always say "well if you didn't smoke…"

Now, the first cigarette of the day started tasting very bad. The second one didn't give much pleasure either. One morning, I got up and as I started to put that cigarette in my mouth, my body said, "Don't do that to me again."

I put the cigarette back in the pack and never smoked another one. I still kept the box in the house, car and work and the three packs on me.

Now, this really broke my heart and I started hating my wife. I had not touched a cigarette for over a month. I never had the urge to smoke. A money issue came up and she started her usual, "If you didn't smoke," I cut her off. I was mad! I put my hands on her shoulders, a very mean look on my face, and I looked her in the eye.

"I haven't smoked a cigarette in over a month and you didn't even notice it. That shows me how much you care for me. Pack up a few things for you and the children. I'll take you to the airport so you can get back to your mommy and daddy. This marriage is over as NOW! I'll pack up the rest of your things and ship them to you."

The divorce settlement stated I was to pay children support, sell the house, and split the money.

So I talked to my then ex-wife, "It's your choice. I keep the house and pay child support or you keep the house and I don't pay child support. She opted to keep the house."

After the divorce, I received a letter from my EX-MIL saying how sorry she was that her daughter couldn't visualize the fantastic life she could have had. I wrote back telling her in my view her daughter doesn't know who she is: straight, heterosexual or lesbian.

I got a letter about a year after the divorce from my ex-wife stating the divorce was the biggest mistake of her life and she misses our dancing and my big cock. I think she finally said something nice about me. She was still asking me to remarry her up until the day she died.

Ok, there was this wife, a mother-in-law, and a nurse and all three. N,o that's not a good start.

Regress: Our marriage was pretty much over while my wife was pregnant with our second daughter. My MIL said she wanted to come out to San Diego when the baby was born. While getting everything together and ready when the baby is born, I told my wife aside from my help during the day with the baby, I'll take care of the baby from midnight until I go to work in the morning. She was so tired by the time we finished dinner, I told her to go to bed. I'll clean up the kitchen and take care of the baby until I go to work. I guess it was about thirty years ago my daughters told me their mother told them I never lifted a hand to help with them. One daughter believes me the other daughter doesn't.

We had the money set aside to replace the money her mom would lose from being off work. Her mother wanted to come out a month before the baby was due. We thought that was a long time but we enjoy her mother and my wife said, her mom needed to get away from her dad for a while.

My wife was sick every day she was pregnant. Her mom and I did all cooking and household chores. After her mother had been here over a week, my wife suggested, "Jim, why don't you take mom out for a while this evening. She needs to get out of the house." Her mom just lit up with excitement. I took her to the Midway

Chuck Wagon. It had a nice buffet and piano bar. As we pulled up in front, she saw the announcement: Buddy Reed at the piano. She gasps!

"That's Regis Philbin's piano player. I don't miss a Regis TV show."

Regis Philbin had a local variety TV show in San Diego. HOLLYWOOD CELIBRITIES, ON THEIR WAYH TO TJ, MEXICO, WOULD UNANNOUNCED JUST WALK ON THE STAGE AND FLABBERGAST REGIS. Christopher Plummer had done that several times.

MIL and I filled our plates, found as table and ordered drinks. Looking around MIL enthralled with the ambiance. We had a great time laughing, joking, drink over dinner. She didn't know what some of the things she was eating, so I was her food guru.

We had another drink, had a desert drink. I ordered Grand Marnier for an after-dinner drink. I asked her if she was ready to go into the piano bar for some dancing.

"I haven't danced with a person that knows how to dance in so long I don't know if I can dance."

Seated at the piano bar MIL was on a high, visiting with Buddy. I didn't know if it was the excitement or the booze. Can we order another one of those grandma things? Sure. We danced a song, stayed for another song, sat for a song sipping drinks. MIL slid off her stool and reached for my hand pulling toward the dance floor. This time she moved in close then pulled me real close.

"I've never been so happy," she whispered.

Seated back on her stool, me standing behind her, she would reach back rubbing my leg. I moved up beside her putting one foot up on the chair rung.

Loud noises coming from the direction of the door.

Buddy Reed said, "Ladies and gentlemen please welcome Mr. Christopher Plummer." I thought MIL would fall off her stool.

The crowd shouted, "Chris sing something for us."

Christopher sang the *Sound of Music* songs. Hazel kept moving her hand against my body.

By this time, she had me excited. She moved her hand down to the inside of my thigh. She moved her hand up, felt the bulge in my pants. She grasped it and her body went stiff. Squeezing the trunk a few times, her body relaxed. I put my hand high up on her leg. I felt a hard squeeze.

"When Christopher leaves, can we go for a walk down by the ocean?"

We left the piano bar, got in my Caddy. As soon as the doors were shut MIL was all over me with full mouth kisses and fingering my crouch. "I've been dying to get you alone for as long as I've known you."

Everything was close. The Chuck Wagon was maybe two miles from the house. The beach was two blocks from the house.

Parked, walking on the beach, it was a dark, cloud covered, and moonless night. Shadowy figures drifted past us. MIL stopped and we put our coats on the ground. We laid down and she started fiddling my belt and zipper.

"Can I help?" I asked.

"No," she said. "This is something I have to do myself. I'm scared, I'm excited."

She touched it and her body gave little jerks and her body froze momentarily. Laying her head beside the throbbing handful, softly murmuring, "This is the hardest thing I've ever done. I've never touched another man's sex organ. I had to do this myself. I wanted to touch yours."

I ran my hand down inside her panties. SURPRISE! An arch de pleasure! As I fingered the opening, legs and body started thrashing and jerking. When the thrashing stopped, she said, "I never knew I could climax that many times in a row."

The wind kicked up.

"Let's go to the car," she said. In the car, I started the engine and turned the heater on.

"Can you find a dark secluded spot? I want to feel you in me."

So MIL, which one of these ten, fifteen places would you like best when I screw you? Which foreplay? Two hands, three holes? Foreskin over the nipples? We'll just be conventional for now.

We went to one of my favorite locations.

"I've driven by here a couple of times. Never seen anyone around."

I stopped the Caddy. She was in the back seat before I got the engine shut off.

She did the guiding. It slid in so easy. Of course, it was pretty well slicked up, felt a little lose. But by now, due to age, they all are.

Putting her panties back on, she said, "I don't have anything with me. I thought if I only had my magic sack."

"Here, this hanky for a manhole cover."

"A WHAT?!" She yelled.

I'm sorry all of sudden it hit me that I hoped the crew picked up the man hole covers so they didn't get stolen and sold for scrap metal.

"How do you feel?" I asked.

"I'm ashamed, guilty. I cheated on my husband. He such a good provider."

"Is he capable of satisfying your physical needs?"

"NO!" was her only response.

"We better get home."

ON the way home MIL laid her head on my lap, holding the love stick against her face, murmuring, "I know it's wrong. But it feels so right. I want to have sex with you every chance I can."

TRIFECTA!

A three-Way Race to the Finish Line!

In the office, I was updating my sex life file, determining which women are immediately within arm's length, for emergency stress relief. I started circling my options. Crossing out non equals, the options began to take shape.

And then it jumped off the page and slapped in the face

Wife circled - last resort
Mother-in-law - anytime
Nurse - Wednesday mornings preferred

Narrowing it down to these three, pondering, reviewing, and working out the logistics, there was this loud voice from inside my pants from an asshole next to my sex advisor.

Wednesday's are TRIFECTA days.

AM: NURSE - SEX AND COFFEE
NOON: MOTHER-IN-LAW – NAKED LUNCH
NIGHT: WIFE – SEX

At work, we had a flex schedule where you worked extended hours and had one day a week off.
Now, which day of the week do you think I choose?
How sad. Wife needed her sleep. I kept my discipline of Wednesdays morning exercise.
My mother-in-law worked out a unique way to let me know anytime it was safe for off the schedule sex. She called it the "**Will you**" game. She would call her daughter. During the causal conversation she would you say, "Before I forget I've got this problem with something…I don't want your father messing with. **Will you** have Jim give me a call?"
Then my wife would say, "I don't want to bother him at work."
But when she does call, I jumped up from my desk and tell my staff, "I got to make a quick run."

SEX RESPONDER ARRIVES

I had a lot of off schedule sex with my MIL. FIL played men's golf every Thursday after work, bowling once a week, called out at night. MIL alone at night, "Daughter, I hear noises, young men running around late at night, I can't get the lights to turn off, lights won't come on. "Can Jim run down here"?

SEXRESPONDER ARRIVES

Our families would go fishing off to the side of the big lake. A sand bar blocked the entrance so you had to pull the boat over it to enter the lake. MIL and I ventured in. On the bank was a big beautiful tree, grass under it. MIL saw it and pointed. We beached the boat. Undressed, and had the most enjoyable sexcapade. Many times I heard her say as she went down to the edge of the water, "I'm gonna' wash up. I don't want any of you in me when we get back to the cabin." We always found a school perch which were very easy to catch, so we could say no luck with keepers.

Every time MIL and I had a chance to go out on the lake together, she would say, "My lake" and point that direction.

The nurse and I had many opportunities for weekends and evening sex as my wife was involved with social activities. Along with some unexpected opportunities I took advantage of.

Nurse, MIL, Wife, TRIFECTA lasted thirteen years.

It was Wednesday's sex times three, unless that period thing got in the way. It ended when I was relocated to San Francisco.

I had sex with MIL and Nurse one more time when I returned for the divorce.

MY MIL was something else. She wanted every hole, crack, and foreplay trick explored to the max. My God! I think if we would have concentrated on it a little more, she would have soon preferred anal sex over vaginal sex.

Oh, San Francisco! Bay area! Great vast surroundings! What a great place to be.

I went to my favorite breakfast restraint in the City. The Omelet Restraint, upstairs at the Cliff House. A place where over the years I've hosted more breakfasts than all the other places I've hosted dinners put together.

I took a small table by the west windows overlooking Seal Rock. The waiter approached. I said, "Bottle of Champagne." He held up two fingers. I held up one.

"Alone," he said kind of sad. I gave him a big, broad smile.

"By choice." Shortly he returned, filled my glass.

"Ready to order?" I placed my hand crossways half up the bottle and nodded. He departed. I sat looking out over the ocean, sipping. I closed my eye, rested my head on the back of the chair. The seals were barking happily as if they were laughing at me. It was like an out of body experience. I was floating on a mythical sea of pussy. Occasionally, through a parting of the pussies, fantastic past partners rose, waving at me, as they drifted off into the heavens as if saying, "I'll be waiting."

The waiter gently touched me on the shoulder, motioning sideways with his hand.

"Number 44." He gave me a thumb's up.

Back in the world of realization, the gentle sound of glasses being lifted and joyful conversations.

My Jonson omelet arrived. "It's nice that with all the evolving the world, some things stay the same." I said to him.

"That Johnny stuffed with crab and avocado with sour cream and sprinkled with sprouts, is the house favorite." He picked up the empty bottle, pointed to it. I shook my head sideways. Eating my 44, I continued the mental conversation with the seals.

I looked around savoring the history of day the sailing ship crashed on the rock and the salvaged lumber used to build the Cliff House.

A past partner wanted to come to SF and most of all she wanted to go to Alcatraz. She had time off in two weeks. I sent her a plane ticket. She was to arrive on a Saturday. I was in a hurry and I ran out of the gym in shorts and tank sweating, cold wind blowing. In the middle of the week I started coming down with a cold. Saturday when she arrived, my cold was full blown. We got her settled in the cold. I said, "Alcatraz here we come."

She said, "No, let's wait until you're feeling better."

My response was, "No, I'd rather be doing something." So off we went.

While touring, we were offered the opportunity to go in a solitary confinement cell to get the feel of what it was for inmates. I jumped at the chance. Standing in that ice-cold, dark room, I leaned my head up against the cold, granite stones. It made my head feel so good I wished I could have stayed longer. An old partner had once told me tequila helped cure colds. By evening, I was feeling pretty good. Or was I drunk?

Contemplating my future situation, I'll go to my breakfast place, talk it over with the seals, see what's floating on the water today. I know they get kinda' loud mouthed at times, but they're honest.

The waiter remembered me. He made a motion like drinking and motioning his hand sideways. I gave him a thumbs up. He raised one finger. I gave him thumbs up. He brought the Champagne, filled my glass, set the bottle down, and placed his hind sideways half way down the side of the bottle. He flashed four fingers twice. I gave him a thumb up. He was a rather large black man. We gave each other big smiles. I got up and gave him a big hug. I said, "Never pass up a chance to keep your mouth shut." He gave me thumbs up and a slap on the back, laughing as he walked away. I yelled after him, "Go ahead, make my day!"

Eating my 44, listening to the seals, gazing over the ocean is the best physiatrist. Thinking out loud, I said, "Got enough time to retire. Where do I want to live? What type work for a second career?"

Some answers started to float to the surface. California, warm, by the ocean, stop the bedding, write a book."

WHERE IN THE HELL DID THAT COME FROM?

San Diego never felt so goooood. Back in the groove! Friday afternoon, tea dance at the Airport Radisson, 50's at the Catamaran Motel in Pacific Beach, shit kickn' at the Abilene Town & Country Motel, Mission Valley, Red Neckn' Lakeside. That'll get me started.

After enjoying San Diego for a couple of years, it was getting to be a hassle dating several women at the same time. Sorting out how to, what to, when to, who to cut, and when to start!!

I selected four women as finalist and cut the rest lose. My plan was to spend extended time with each one, trip and living.

When it came down to earth day-to-day living, the cracks in the "Chosen Ones" (I don't mean naked from the waist down), started floating to the surface, all except one.

Every morning getting out of bed she was happy, contented, and positive. Daily grind didn't faze her. She liked doing all the varied things I liked. Never patronizing, up for anything from conventional sex with all the foreplay, excellent cook and house keeper, great traveler, great dancer, conversationalist, up on all current events, excellent hygiene habits, has hobbies, and reads.

So we moved in together. Every morning, the same thing was foremost on both our minds,

"WHAT CAN I DO TODAY FOR MY PARTNER TO MAKE LIFE EASIER?"

There was nothing in the house that was gender specific. If something needed to be done, DO IT!!!
The gal I moved in with, her husband divorced her after a thirty-year marriage. I'm glad he did.

As final test, I took her to San Francisco. I told her we'll be together 24/7 and if we're both still alive, I'd like us live together.

During the flight, I told her, "I want to make sure you know I'm paying for everything. But here's a hundred-dollar bill. If you see something for remembrance, buy it for yourself."

MY CITY! Leaving the airport in the rental car, I did not go right to the hotel. I drove north on Van Ness to Lombard Street, U turn left for the Golden Gate Bridge. I tuned right up the hill. When we got to Hyde Street, I stopped the car and told Gerry, "You drive. When you cross over Hyde you'll have the greatest view of the city." She crested the hill, slammed on the breaks screaming SHIT! She was looking down the curviest street in the world. I told her we'll just sit here a few, take some deep breathes, when you're comfortable, take your time and slowly drive down.

We dropped our bags in the room.

"I know a great place to view the city." I said.

We went to Treasure Island. There is a bar with plate glass windows that faces the city. We sat at a table right in front of the windows. I ordered a bottle of Champagne. She questioned it as it was only 11:00 am.

"Trust me." I said.

Our view was from the Bay Bridge to Alcatraz and the Golden Gate Bridge, with San Francisco skyline across the bay. I was pleased watching her excitement. Sipping, pointing out and answering her questions.

"What a first day."

"You sound like you're satisfied and want to go to the hotel. We won't get to the hotel until about 11:00 p.m. Too many things to do today."

It was lunch time. I told Gerry, "We'll go ever to Fishermen's Warf."

Gerry looked at the menu posted on the wall, "I don't know what to have?"

"They have the world's best clam chowder. I'm having that in a sour dough bread bowl."

"What's that? Gerry asked.

"See these round loafs of bread? They cut the tops off, hollow it out and fill it with soup of choice. Eat the soup, eat the bowl."

"Sounds good. I'll have that also." She said.

After lunch, we did Pier 39 and waked the wharf. I looked at my watch.

"Four fifteen. Let's head for the Holiday Inn. At five, the Friday afternoon tea dance starts. They have a great 50s rock-and-roll band. It's on the second floor, above the hotel entrance. And man, that place gets packed and it's jumping."

We felt the floor moving up and down. We were in heaven. The dance ended at seven.

Gerry asked, "Are we going to have dinner here?"

"After we get some fresh air, I have a special place where I'm cooking dinner for you."

"I've never had so much fun."

"Well, I thought we did pretty well in San Diego."

Gerry asked, "If you're cooking, where's the grocery store?"

"Where we're going they have all I need." I replied.

"What kind of place is it?" was her curiously question.

"Trust me, you'll like it," was my reply.

Found a parking place. Walking down the street, I stopped at a store that had Tartan Scottish clothing in the window with the name Edinburg Castle on the front of the building.

"This is the place." I announced.

Gerry looked puzzled. "I know. It's that trust thing," she said laughing.

Entering, the first thing you see is a myna bird that talks to you. Gerry just stood, taking in the ambience of this quant Scottish bar. Gerry took a step toward a booth. I stopped her, pointing to the bar. Gerry ordered wine and I, my special - three fingers Knob Creek, two cubes and a splash. Gerry looking around, "I don't see any kitchen?"

"They don't have one." I said.

"How you going to," she stopped, "I know, trust you."

I flashed two fingers at the bar tender and gave chewing motion.

A kid came running the back door with two small bundles of newspaper. The bartender put them down in front of us.

I turned to Gerry, "Viola, dinner is served."

The aroma of the fish n' chips made us feeling starved instantly. I picked up a bottle and shook it over the fish. I handed the bottle to Gerry.

"Malt vinegar."

Gerry said while she was eating, "You cooked a fantastic dinner."

"The original Fish n" Chips place is just down the street." I told her.

The Bag Piper came down the stairs in full dress. Marched up and down, playing, and it was off the scale for Gerry.

"Every Thursday nights they have a piper jam session upstairs."

Back at the hotel, we stripped naked and after the bathroom routine, we crawled in bed.

Gerry said, "What a fantastic first day. I love your city."

Today, at age 80, we still sleep naked!

Morning coffee was served in our room. There was a knock on the door, "Room service."

Gerry still in bed went to get up. I stopped her.

"Pull the covers up to your neck."

I got my robe, opened the door, coffee was set on the table. Server left. I moved Gerry's coffee to her night stand. "Welcome to a day of adventure."

"Are you going to cook breakfast?" she asked.

"Yes, I am."

Gerry said, "I can only guess."

"We have to drive to the kitchen."

It was pleasant driving through Golden State Park. Parked at the Cliff House, Gerry was taking in the sights.

Entering the Omelet Restaurant, the greeter acknowledged us. I flashed four fingers twice and two fingers, put one palm over the other about a foot apart.

The greater said, "two Johnson's and a bottle of champagne."

I said, "Right, and a table at the west windows."

It was like Gerry was having an out of body experience.

Gerry said, "How could ever leave the city?"

"I love it," I said. "But it's too cold."

After breakfast, we spent a little time in the museum, which is part of the Cliff House complex, looking at the San Quentin prisoner arts and crafts work.

"Can we have breakfast here every day?"

"No! Tomorrow we have to get up early. We're taking a Champagne hot air balloon ride at sun up, over the wine vineyards of Napa Valley."

Gerry was ecstatic. "I've always wanted to take a Hot air balloon ride."

Just the high lights: Walked the Golden Gate Bridge, Oakland's Jack London Square for drink at the tilted bar, Winchester House, Renaissance Fair at Black Point, state Scottish Highland games at Santa Rosa, shit kick n' at Marin County style at Marty's on hill in Sebastopol, sitting beside the dance floor eating Calms Casino and Oysters Rockefeller. Placerville, Thomas Kincaid's first studio, Sutter's Mill (gold discovery), Coloma to see Wyatt Earp's grave, dinner bay cruise, Fiolluly House, Sausalito, shit kickn' at San Leandro.

Sex was the least important thing on our minds.

Gerry does San Francisco over, leaving for the airport early, we took the high scenic route. We stopped at a small café, and because the door was open we went in.

Bartender said, "We're not open yet."

"Just looking for some breakfast."

"What do you want? If it's not too fancy, I can maybe fix you something."

"Just some ham and eggs."

"I can do that," bartender replied.

Gerry's mood quiet and withdrawn.

"Happy and sad. So many memories. Will we ever come back?"

We did it twice!

Now at age eighty and thirty-two years later, Esther (Gerry) Dye and I are still very happy living together. Naked, she looked at herself in the mirror and asked, "How do I look!?

"Just has beautiful as the first time I pulled your panties off!" was my reply.

DO'S AND DON'T'S of living together. WE DO NOT MIX MONEY! We share all household expense, chores, cooking, and grocery shopping.

The only thing we don't have in common: she likes to go out and eat. I do not. She has her Red Hats, Quilting gals, lunch-bunch gals. I'll gladly spend $200 and prepare us a meal at home. I make sure she has always plenty of money on the Starbucks card I gave her years ago and an ongoing fully charged, never ending, gift certificate for her salon.

Me, I grew up on a farm. I worked on a farm as a hired man for the four years I was in High school. Fast food was, if you work around the buildings, you got hungry, you'd go up to the house, grab a couple slices of bread, without PB&J, and eat on the go. If you were doing field work, the wife would bring you a cheese sandwich and a pint of milk.

All my working life, I could be running around town, pocked full of money. And when I get hungry, I go home and have a bowl of cereal. Driving around town, the sweet smell of baking and BBQ smell, almost makes me sick. Just the thought of taking money out of my pocket to give to someone for fast food, I get a warm, burning sensation, on the tips of my fingers.

When I sat down to write the TRUE SEX exposé, it would have been easier if I had kept a FUCKING JOURNAL.

Coming to the end trek through my world of sex, I'll follow Andy Rooney's lead. Andy was a WW II correspondent and a syndicated journalist. Andy felt the only way to write with the feeling of the air war was flying in a B 17 on a bombing run over Germany. Only then could he write with the sense of observing, hearing, smell and the anxiety of the flight crew and put his readers in the cockpit on a bombing run.

I looked, poked, smelled into every hole and crack. The things sticking out that drew an interest, and sucked out the story.

My favorite Andy saying **: Life is like a roll of toilet paper. The closer you get to the end, the faster it goes.**

REST IN PEACE ANDY ROOMEY

How do I want my life to end? You always hear a lot about lines. Life line, draw the line, underline, and jump the line.

The only line I want to see is the RED line the needle of the tachometer pointing to the dashboard of my Corvette as if I'm in a full sideways drift, dumped into the fires of HELL, yelling 'HOLLY SHIT, WHAT A RIDE!"

As my soul drifts up, out of the clouds, becoming aware of my surroundings, ending in front of the person in charge saluting and saying, "THE REAL POPE HAS ARRIVED! I HAVE THE CON!SHOVE OFF! GRAB A CLOUD."

Surveying my new surroundings, all my past partners came drifting by, each on their own cloud, blowing kisses, waving, and motioning for me. I found myself in my old Corvette. On the passenger seat was the MAGIC SACK.

The GPS lit up and locked on. The car mystically started in motion, blasting to WARP4, accelerating towards the first cloud of the CLOUD TRIP.

As Bugs Bunny would say
Da,Da,DA, dat's all folks!

To para-phrase Jeff Foxworthy:
You may be a sewer RAT if:
You call the VIRGINA a HANHOLE, the PAD a MANHOLE COVER

Words of wisdom from an old diesel boat submariner:
SEX IS LIKE AIR! YOU MISS IT UNTIL YOUR NOT GET N' ANY!

Printed in the United States
by Baker & Taylor Publisher Services